Chapter 7

Getting the Socks Picked Up: Parenting 101

Everybody knows how to raise children,
except people who have them.

P. J. O'ROURKE, *THE BACHELOR HOME COMPANION*

Not every parenting struggle you face is due to living in a stepfamily. Sometimes it's just the natural challenges of parenting.

"We team up well as parents," said Troy. "I work hard to support my wife in her role with my children and she supports me with hers. But what's the best way to discipline? For example, we are trying to get them to pick up their clothes and be responsible for themselves, but we don't seem to be getting anywhere. What are we doing wrong?"

Troy's question is insightful, as it reveals two key aspects of parenting: process and behavioral management. The *process* of parenting and stepparenting involves how you work together and the underlying dynamics of the family. I discussed these aspects of parenting in detail in chapters 5 and 6. One example is for mothers to take the primary disciplinary role with their children early on while the stepfather builds much-needed relationship and respect with them. A stepdad's authoritative role is tentative in the beginning and requires firm support from his wife. Another process principle I discussed is for parents to be on the same team and united regarding the boundaries and rules. Troy and his wife were applying those principles well, but they still struggled with the daily *behavioral management* of their children. Their parenting questions centered on how to properly motivate the children to be responsible and how to discipline them effectively if they didn't obey.

> ## Befriending Adult Stepchildren
>
> With adult stepchildren your goal is not to increase parental authority, but to find a mutually suitable friendship. If your stepchildren were adults when you first entered their lives, read this chapter thinking of how you might apply the principles with your stepgrandchildren.

In this chapter I'd like to offer a brief tutorial on behavioral management in parenting. The strategies offered here are equally helpful for both you and your wife, because the more you work together, the more effective the results. Understanding and implementing the process principles of parenting is a must before implementing the strategies in this chapter, so it is worth repeating: Read chapters 5 and 6 prior to this chapter. Much of what you will read here will not work if you haven't applied the process principles of parenting and stepparenting first.

The ages of your stepchildren, and whether you are a part- or full-time stepfamily, will influence how many and which of the following strategies will work. Talk with your wife and decide together how to proceed.

PARENTING: WHAT'S THE GOAL?

Our job as parents and stepparents is to work ourselves out of a job. In other words, we want to instill within our children an internal compass that guides them to make godly decisions, and

"At Focus on the Family, we routinely hear from fathers facing the challenges associated with remarriage and living in a blended family. *The Smart Stepdad* is like a lifeline to these men—and to their wives, as well—with practical advice and biblical counsel."
Jim Daly
President, Focus on the Family

"To climb Stepdad Mountain you need a climbing guide; Ron Deal and this book are it. Get started."
Dr. Kevin Leman
Author of *Have a New Kid by Friday*

"*The Smart Stepdad* sheds a bright light on the unique challenges of being a stepdad. Your role is vital to your family and this book can help you find success."
John Rosemond
Family psychologist
Author of *The Well-Behaved Child: Discipline That Really Works!*

"Finally!!! This book is long overdue. It is an absolute must-read for any stepdad or man who is dating a woman with children. Ron has given a very clear map for success for men who are in one of the most important positions in the kingdom."
Dr. Chuck Stecker
President / Founder of A Chosen Generation

The Smart Stepdad

Ron L. Deal

BETHANYHOUSE
Minneapolis, Minnesota

Published by Bethany House Publishers
11400 Hampshire Avenue South
Bloomington, Minnesota 55438

Bethany House Publishers is a division of
Baker Publishing Group, Grand Rapids, Michigan.

Printed in the United States of America

Library of Congress Cataloging-in-Publication Data

Deal, Ron L.
The smart stepdad : steps to help you succeed / Ron L. Deal.
    p. cm.
Includes bibliographical references.
Summary: "Encouragement and practical advice for stepdads from a leading stepfamily expert. Includes parenting advice, chapters for wives to read, tips for relating to adult stepchildren, and discussion questions"—Provided by publisher.
    ISBN 978-0-7642-0696-2 (pbk. : alk. paper) 1. Stepfathers. 2. Remarried people—Family relationships. I. Title.
    HQ759.92.D39   2011
    306.874'7—dc22
                                                            2010041144

In keeping with biblical principles of creation stewardship, Baker Publishing Group advocates the responsible use of our natural resources. As a member of the Green Press Initiative, our company uses recycled paper when possible. The text paper of this book is comprised of 30% post-consumer waste.

11   12   13 · 14   15   16   17   8   7   6   5   4   3   2

DEDICATION

To my dad—
mentor, teacher, and coach in what matters most—baayo.

To all the stepdads
who are striving to be a mentor, teacher, and coach to another man's child.

And to the heavenly Father—
thank you for adopting us us your sons and daughters
and teaching us the heart-softening power
of stubborn, determined love.

Books by
Ron L. Deal

The Remarriage Checkup (with David H. Olson)

The Smart Stepdad

The Smart Stepfamily

The Smart Stepfamily Small Group Resource (DVD)

The Smart Stepmom (with Laura Petherbridge)

an internal hard drive that results in responsible, self-motivated behavior. We pray that they will become capable, responsible adults who are sensitive to the needs of others. And as Christians we desire that they find their fulfillment and purpose in Jesus.

Effective parenting requires a long-term perspective on the development of the child. We aren't just trying to get the socks picked up; we are trying to create responsible children who understand the value of caring for their possessions.

Therefore, discipline strategies should be aimed at the long-term goal of building the internal hard drive of the child. On occasion, discipline uses *power tactics* to change immediate behavior. For the most part, however, parenting should attempt to *empower* the child to learn lessons that shape his internal hard drive; these lessons will extend well into the future and prepare him for life. For example, yelling at a nine-year-old to clean his room (power tactic) will likely result in immediate behavior, but what has the child learned? That his stepdad gets angry and the only way to calm him down is to clean his room? Wouldn't it be better to teach responsibility by giving him or her the choice of cleaning the room before or after dinner, and then holding the child accountable for following through? This method teaches self-initiative and personal responsibility, which moves the child a step toward cleaning the room without someone else's initiative. (And just as important, this strategy reminds a stepdad that calming himself down is his job, not the child's.)

Let's contrast the two styles further.

> **For Mom**
>
> Research affirms that initially your remarriage and the adjustments of living in a stepfamily may bring about increased conflict between you and your children. But stay the course. Over time, conflict decreases to normal levels and your relationship with your kids might even improve compared to the single-parent years.[1]

Power parents *take control* of their kids (e.g., "Do it now"); empowering parents *take charge* of their children (e.g., "Will you clean your room before or after dinner?").[2] Empowering parents are like the highway department. On a multi-lane freeway they don't tell you which lane you must drive in or how fast you must go (power tactics), but they do mark the right and left boundaries (with solid white and double yellow lines) and put limits on your speed. Within the boundaries, you have lots of freedom and choice; cross a boundary, however, and you will pay the price. Effective parents strive for this environment in their home.

FIVE PRINCIPLES OF EFFECTIVE DISCIPLINE

With a long-term empowering perspective, let's explore five key principles for effective behavioral management of children and teens.

Rooted in Love

God loved us even before he made us, but he had to make us to prove it.

CHILD, IN *KIDS SAY THE GREATEST THINGS ABOUT GOD*

Do you know what makes God's discipline tolerable? His relentless love. Hebrews 12:5–11 tells us that God disciplines those he loves. His motive is holiness; he is trying to shape us into the image of his Son. When we understand his reason for discipline, the chastisement becomes bearable. Put another way, we know God has our best in mind when he lowers the boom. Your stepchildren need to be constantly reminded of your love for them. If they doubt your motives, your authority will be questioned.

Consider the matter of helping children find their strengths. It communicates love when you help kids mature into their own God-given unique abilities, not the ones you wish they had. My wife, Nan, speaks of the dangers of cookie-cutter parenting. Like cookies made during the holidays, cookie-cutter parents assume all children are comprised of the same shape, size, and ability. They are not. If anything, children may be cut out in a similar shape, but how God has decorated them makes each uniquely different. It's our job as parents to identify God's decoration and encourage development. Some children have a natural bent toward athletics, others enjoy music, and others are gifted in the arts. Helping a child identify his or her strengths and then exploring opportunities that might enhance the talent is an act of love. This makes a child feel special and reveals that you care.

Learning a child's love language is another way to demonstrate love. In his bestselling book *The Five Love Languages,*[3] Gary Chapman shares that everyone has a primary way of expressing and receiving love. Typically, an individual uses one of five possible languages. Most people appreciate all five types, but one frequently communicates love more loudly than the others. Some children prefer to hear words of affirmation such as "I love you" or "You are a blessing to my life." Another child might prefer receiving gifts, either purchased or handmade. For the child who prefers meaningful touch, a hug, holding hands, or soft touches on the arm convey that you care. A message of love in this kinesthetic language is heard loud and clear. Fourth, engaging a child in activities or conversation are two examples of how to communicate love to the child who spells love *t-i-m-e*. Lastly, some children receive love through acts of service such as kindness, taking care of tasks, and/or serving their needs.

How can you know which love language your stepchildren speak? The first rule of thumb is to notice how they express love to others. I have one child who, for example, from a young age made pictures for me. His face would beam when giving them to me; he obviously felt that he was showing me love with the present. Guess how he most wants to receive love: gifts. I have another child who is quick to articulate love (words of affirmation) and another who enjoyed (he died at the age of twelve) building Lego's together (quality time). All children need to hear love through each channel, but make sure you know what language to speak when it really counts.

Whenever Possible, Let Reality Be the Teacher

Upon a recent visit to Washington, D.C., I learned that you cannot park your car along the National Mall (bordering the White House, U. S. Capitol, Washington Memorial, and Lincoln Memorial) after 4:00 p.m. How did I learn that? I got a parking ticket. Reality is always the best teacher for both adults and children.[4] There are a number of ways to let reality teach.

Natural consequences are the innate outcomes of a child's behavior. If a child goes out in the rain without a coat, they get wet. If they forget their basketball shoes, like one of my sons did one afternoon, and don't realize it until you have driven across town to their practice, then they practice in their bare feet. (After all, it is not my job to rescue him from the natural consequence of forgetting.) Natural consequences are great opportunities for children to learn. In other words, sometimes the best thing you can do as a parent is to do nothing. Allow the child to learn from their own mistakes.

Jason waited till 9:00 p.m. the night before his science project was due to tell his stepdad, Craig, that he needed items from the store. He neglected the project till the last minute and then expected his stepdad to help out. Craig thought about it for a minute and replied, "I'm sorry that you've waited till now to tell me this. You've had three weeks to work on the project. Just because you have decided to act irresponsibly does not mean I should jump in and fix the problem for you. Jason, you're a smart kid and I want you to do well in school. But I'm not going to bail you out this time. I'm sure you can figure something out." And with that, he cut him loose to experience the consequences of procrastination.

Parents sometimes wonder if they are being cruel to let children experience this type of consequence. They are not. They are preparing the child to accept responsibility for their choices. In addition, they are inviting the child to teach themselves how to manage their responsibilities.

Let us pause for an important reminder: Your ability to take action similar to Craig—or implement any of the strategies in this chapter—assumes that you and your wife agree that allowing a child to suffer a consequence when they make a poor choice is a valuable disciplinary tool. If your wife would not respond in this way, your decision to act in this manner will be challenged. You can still respond in this manner, but it might bring a negative response from your wife (which, by the way, doesn't mean you did the wrong thing). Having similar parenting philosophies is vital. If you currently disagree on what is effective parenting, read this chapter together and discuss which strategies you will utilize.

Logical consequences involve consequences imposed by the parent as a result of the child's behavior. If a child spills their milk, they should clean it up (whether two years old, with some help, or twenty-three). If they agree to finish their chores before dinner and do not, they should not be allowed to eat supper until the chores are completed. If they stay out past their curfew, they should be docked time the next night (or if a pattern has developed, not be allowed to go out at all). We might refer to this as "if—then" consequences: if you do this, then you get that.

Providing choices or setting boundaries is another example of logical consequences. "Would you rather finish your homework before or after your favorite TV show?" (Notice that doing homework is not an option, just when they do it.) "Would you rather clean your room or pay your sister with your allowance to do it for you?" Giving choices, even to two-year-olds, is an important part of long-term training. Children learn to schedule their time in order to fulfill commitments, they learn to plan ahead, and they learn to make choices with money instead of having a parent tell them what to do. Just like when the highway department paints yellow and white lines restricting our

> **Stepdad Wisdom**
>
> Letting natural consequences occur is a wise, safe response for "baby-sitter" stepdads, while "uncle" and "parent mentor" stepdads can implement logical consequences.

driving, your job and Mom's is to set the boundaries for the children's choices and then enforce consequences if the child does not drive within the lanes.

Robert and his wife, Natalie, let her sixteen-year-old son, Caleb, decide if he was going to play football and serve on the youth praise band at the same time. They made it clear to him that if he chose to do so and his grades suffered, he would lose access to his cell phone and leisure computer time. When the six-weeks grades came in, it was clear to everyone that his grades had suffered. But when it came time to impose the consequence, Natalie decided that Caleb could use a second chance; she rescinded the consequence. This angered Robert because he felt that it was teaching Caleb that choices don't have consequences (and it was). It also hurt him because he felt that their agreement wasn't being honored. After a few days of discussion, Natalie realized that she needed to follow through on the consequence. Caleb was very angry and blamed the punishment on Robert. Thankfully, Natalie was strong enough to tell her son that she was the one who decided to enforce the consequences, not Robert.

Talk Less, Act More[5]

Parents today use too many words. We have this silly idea that if we talk long enough, our children will finally agree with what we believe is best for them and then gladly obey. It really is funny when you see it in print, huh?

"Why can't I go to the movie, Samuel? All the other kids in my grade have seen it!" Samuel had just explained to his stepson Hayden that he could not go to the PG-13 movie. "I don't care if everyone has seen it. Your mother and I have talked about this and our rule is that we preview all movies before you see them. Besides, you're ten and it's unlikely that we'll let you start seeing movies like that until you're at least thirteen. Your mother and I have told you this before; our decision is not based on age, but on the content of the film. If it isn't healthy for your soul, you're not going to see the movie." Hayden fired back with anger: "This isn't fair!"

Let's analyze this situation. The phrase "I've told you this before" reveals that this isn't the first time this issue has come up. So it's time to stop talking (i.e., trying to get Hayden to be happy about this) and do something.

Children need to know our values and how decisions are made. That's how they learn what matters in life and how values impact the way we live. Therefore, talking or *teaching* is an important element of parenting. But once the teaching is over, if the child continues to badger, argue, complain, or misbehave, it's no longer time to talk. It's time to act.

In this case, Hayden continued to badger Samuel. "But that's not fair . . . Why can't I go . . . You don't love me." So Samuel took action. "I have explained this to you. You can continue to argue with me if you'd like, but from this point forward, every time you complain it will cost you five dollars of your allowance," and with that said he walked away (signaling the end of the discussion). Taking charge of yourself and the situation is empowered, self-defined leadership. And it goes a long way toward training children to respect others, work within the boundaries of life, and take responsibility for themselves.

By the way, how do you know it's time to stop talking and act? One way is to apply the mall test. Imagine describing the child's behavior to a hundred people at a mall. What percentage of them would say, "Yeah, that crosses the line. It's time to do something different"? Your anger or resentment toward a stepchild may have taught you to distrust your emotions. The mall test helps to objectively examine the situation and then decide how to proceed. If you're really not sure, withhold action till you have discussed it with your wife.

Catch Them Doing Something Right

Encouraging appropriate behavior is a very effective discipline strategy. It is so easy to notice inappropriate or negative behavior because it catches our attention. What is not as obvious is when children obey, follow through, consider others first, or make the choice to do the *right* thing. Set a standard of what you'd like to see in the children, not merely what you want to experience less, and then draw attention to it.

Think about the last genuine compliment you received—or perhaps a performance raise at work. How did it impact you? Likely it encouraged you to press on (or keep up your efforts), put a smile on your face, and felt good way down deep inside. This is the power of encouragement. Build others up, Paul commends in Ephesians 4:29, "according to their needs, that it may benefit those who listen." Notice that we each have a need to be built up (and at times may have a particular area that needs attention). Children in particular have a need to know that what they are doing meets your expectations. This brings a smile to their face (just like your last raise at work brought a smile to yours). It also has the bonus impact for a stepdad of facilitating closeness with a stepchild.

Brooke's stepdad, Danny, was an encourager. A young professional now living on her own, Brooke reflected on her childhood. "Danny believed in me when I didn't believe in myself," she shared. "When I went through those awkward adolescent years and I didn't think anyone cared for me, he always found something in me to compliment. And when I wanted to quit taking violin lessons, he gently insisted I keep going because, as he said, I 'had so much potential.' I lived off his confidence for a long time."

Catching them doing something right includes commenting on inner qualities, not just outward performance. For example, a straight-A report card could be celebrated as "You're so smart." But it would be even more effective to say, "You obviously applied yourself this semester; you worked hard and it paid off. Congratulations!" The former celebrates the outcome (which might communicate conditional approval that pressures a similar performance in the future). The latter celebrates the inner drive that led to the good grades. It is that quality you want to reinforce, even if a future outcome isn't necessarily the same.

Consider how you might "encourage forward" your stepchild as a way to help him or her move closer to the desired goal. This is the "glass half empty or half full" aspect of catching them doing it right. For example, on your way out the door to school, you could make a "half empty" scowling comment to your eight-year-old: "You forgot to make your lunch again. Why can't you remember to do that?" Rather, try to make a "half full" observation: "We leave in two minutes and I noticed something this morning. You have made your bed, put away your dishes, brushed your teeth, and gathered your backpack for school all without having to be reminded. Amazing! You rock! Now, I'm wondering if you have everything you need for the day . . . ?" This praise of the child's steps offers encouragement and a subtle invitation for the child to think through what they need, rather than having to be told to get their lunch. It focuses on what is going well while moving the child toward further responsibility.

A related strategy that I like to call solution-oriented parenting calls attention to the child's ability to find resolution for a situation. "Nicely done. How did you know to do that?" is a question that celebrates the child's behavior but more importantly declares them competent. This translates into self-esteem. "I noticed your brother was really pestering you today—getting into your stuff without asking and trying to push your buttons. But you didn't lose your cool. What went on inside you that helped to manage your emotions and do the right thing?" This observation and question offers a compliment and an invitation for the child to reflect and learn.

Solution-oriented parenting invites the child to figure out what they should do to resolve a dilemma (which is better for long-term training than telling them). Upon learning that a middle-school child, for example, isn't managing their study time well, a parent could overreact: "You can't leave your room until your grades are better." Or instead, the parent could ask a question and let the child find a plausible solution: "What will you do differently when you are making better use of your time?" The discussion that follows creates an action plan that originates with the child's input. This is much more likely to be carried out and might alleviate the problem. If the child continues to mismanage time, the next parenting phase might be to impose a logical consequence that restricts them from spending time with friends while focusing on their studies. Keep in mind this rule of thumb: It is better to encourage a child's learning and problem-solving skills before imposing external controls.

What's Not in the List

You'll notice that criticism, name calling, yelling, bribing, pleading, and manipulative threatening didn't make my recommended list of parenting strategies. That's because these harsh strategies can negatively impact a child's spirit. These tactics are tempting because they give the appearance of working, and they can halt inappropriate behavior. But *power strategies* only work for the short term. They do not mold a critical internal hard drive that prepares children for mature living.

There are moments when a parent must immediately change a child's behavior. For example, when a three-year-old is about to walk into the street, or when an older brother is wrestling with a younger sibling and he doesn't realize that his strength is hurting the child. In those circumstances, a non-critical power strategy—like speaking loudly—is necessary to take control. But recognize the training limits of this response. It will bring about immediate safety but will not equip your stepchildren for life. It's best to utilize empowerment strategies liberally and power strategies conservatively.

In addition, these harsh strategies require a high degree of parental status. If someone you really love and admire calls you spoiled, it hurts, but forgiveness is possible. If someone you don't know very well calls you a name, it's much more difficult to work through (see again the chapters discussing attachment and loyalty). When a stepdad has a fragile relationship with a stepchild and he implements harsh discipline, it fractures the relationship and ignites your wife's need to defend and protect her kids. This pushes you further to the outside and undercuts any gains in authority.

Putting It All Together

Discipline and punishment bring to the surface many of the concepts mentioned throughout this book. Here are some thoughts as you put it all together.

- Issues of loss and loyalty are usually at play. When you impose punishment, you test your level of authority in the child's heart (see chapter 5), remind them of their losses (see chapter 3), and possibly ignite a child's internal loyalty conflicts (see chapter 4). There is always more going on than meets the eye.

- You and your wife should not let these realities paralyze you (chapter 6). A loving but firm follow-through is needed.

- Each of the strategies in this chapter has pros and cons. Find what works with each individual child, in this season of life, and use it. Often this requires a "try it and see" approach. Be sure you and your wife talk frequently about what seems to work best with each child.

- Above all, you and your wife must be a team in order to lead your family. Follow the Parental Unity Rules (chapter 5).

A WORK IN PROGRESS

Parenting is a work in progress. We should never stop learning how to parent. This chapter is meant as a primer on parenting, not an exhaustive discourse on the subject. I strongly encourage you and your wife to read books (some recommended resources follow), attend parenting classes and seminars, and keep open a dialogue about how you will parent your children. The more you learn, the better you will function in your God-given role.

God doesn't expect you to be perfect as a parent, just good enough. Be sure to pray constantly about your role. God, our heavenly Father, understands about raising children and is more than happy to offer wisdom for every circumstance.

Recommended Reading

These books do not specifically address stepparenting dynamics, but they offer solid teaching on discipline and child rearing.

- Dr. Kevin Leman, *Making Children Mind Without Losing Yours* (Grand Rapids, MI: Revell, 2000).

- John Rosemond, *Parenting by The Book* (New York: Howard Books, 2007).

- Foster Cline and Jim Fay, *Parenting with Love and Logic: Teaching Children Responsibility* (Colorado Springs, CO: Pinion Press, 2006).

- Foster Cline and Jim Fay, *Parenting Teens with Love and Logic: Preparing Adolescents for Responsible Adulthood* (Colorado Springs, CO: Pinion Press, 1992).

- Dr. James Dobson, *The New Dare to Discipline* (Wheaton, IL: Tyndale, 1992).

- Cynthia Ulrich Tobias, *You Can't Make Me (But I Can Be Persuaded): Strategies for Bringing Out the Best in Your Strong-Willed Child* (Colorado Springs, CO: Waterbrook Press, 1999).

HEROES BY CHOICE

For Group Discussion

1. In this chapter I state that "our job as parents and step-parents is to work ourselves out of a job." This is a long-term perspective. When you make parenting decisions, do you tend to think more short term or long term?

2. What's the difference between trying to *take control* of your children and stepchildren and trying to *take charge* of them? (Keep in mind that because of a strong attachment, it is easier for biological parents to *take control* when they need to; stepparents must step lightly in this arena.)

3. Would your stepchildren say that you love them?

4. Think of each of your stepchildren. What is their primary love language?

   Words of affirmation
   Gifts
   Meaningful touch
   Time together
   Acts of service

5. Whenever possible, let reality be the teacher. List some natural and logical consequences that have worked with your stepchildren. What hasn't worked?

6. Review the principle Talk Less, Act More. Why do you think we try to talk our children into better behavior? Are you or your wife more likely to keep talking to the kids?

7. Share how you try to "catch" your stepkids doing something right. When someone does that for you, how does it encourage you?

8. List and discuss some items that did not make the top strategies for behavior management list (see page 130). Do you need to resist using some of these?

9. Review the Putting It All Together sidebar on page 131. How does being aware of the various dynamics at play help you to make better decisions as a stepdad?

10. Parenting is a work in progress. What next steps can you take to improve your parenting (for example, taking a class or reading one of the recommended books)?

Chapter 8

Meet Your Ex-Husband-in-Law: Friend or Foe?

In some ways his actions make me look like a hero. He is manipulative, talks bad about their mother in front of them, and is undependable. My role is to remain loving and keep my mouth shut when "all hell is breaking loose." I want to let them experience an alternative way of fathering in the hope that they have a better role model to carry into the future.

TIM

I have a better relationship with him than my wife does! I try to be very careful not to violate his relationship with the kids—even though I don't think he's the best dad. You have to respect that "blood thing."

BOB

The Serenity Prayer by Reinhold Niebuhr states, "God, grant me the serenity to accept the things I cannot change; courage to change the things I can; and wisdom to know the difference." Here is a truth you cannot change: When you marry a divorced woman, you acquire a mother-in-law, father-in-law, and as I like to say, an ex-husband-in-law.* I hope this chapter will help provide some much-needed wisdom to discern what you can change and what you can't regarding his role in your life and family. As I said in my first book, *The Smart Stepfamily*, divorce doesn't end family life, it just reorganizes it. Your girlfriend or wife is an ex-spouse but never an ex-parent. Forever, she and you, her kids . . . and *he* are "extended family" to one another. In other words, your ex-husband-in-law is on Stepdad Mountain and will either help or hinder your climb. Learning how to turn your interaction with him into an asset instead of dead weight will make a world of difference in your ascent. So let's figure out how to make the best of it.

> ### When Dad Is Deceased
>
> A deceased father is still a member of your family; therefore, this chapter still applies to you. His memory is part of the family story and very important to your wife and her children. This chapter can help you to explore the character traits of your deceased husband-in-law and how his memory might impact your family.

THE GOAL

The primary goal of managing your relationship with the father of your stepchildren is to bring a blessing to the kids. Sure, a mutually respectful relationship reduces stress and advances your role as stepdad, but the primary purpose is to facilitate peace for the children. The more harmony there is between homes, the more your stepchildren are free to live, love, and grow. Research clearly shows that children who have a positive relationship with both their father and stepfather fare better emotionally, academically, economically, and psychologically.[1] By contrast, ongoing conflict between homes is highly predictive of

---

*This chapter also applies if a woman was never married to the child's father (an out-of-wedlock birth).

negative outcomes for children on almost every measure[2] (this includes conflict both between your wife and her ex-husband and between you and him). This doesn't have to be. Of course, conflict is a two-way street and you can't control how your ex-husband-in-law behaves, but "as far as it depends on you, live at peace" (Romans 12:18).

There are many other reasons to have an amicable or even better—cooperative—relationship with your ex-husband-in-law.

- Conflict tempts fathers to disengage from their children. As I'll discuss further, deactivated dads cause harm to children, and then everyone loses.

- Conflict automatically pulls children into the emotional tug-of-war discussed in chapter 4.

- Planning and cooperation between homes becomes more difficult when animosity abounds. For example, trying to negotiate simple drop-off or pick-up tasks becomes very complicated, not to mention planning detailed events like family vacations or holiday schedules.

- The more hostile and anxious the climate between homes, the more marginalized you become with your stepchildren. In chapter 4, I discussed how your stepchildren not only have to figure out how to accept, respect, and love you, they have to learn how to do so in a way that doesn't make them feel disloyal to their father. In general, the more conflict between you and him, the more children feel compelled to stand in opposition to you. That's why giving the No-Threat Message is so important.

THE NO-THREAT MESSAGE

In chapter 4, I gave an example of the No-Threat Message as it relates to children and loyalty conflicts, but it needs repeating here relative to your ex-husband-in-law. Biological fathers resent being challenged in their role as a dad. In order to make it clear to both him and his children that you are not trying to take his

Smart Dating

A biological dad may not show his true colors until you are married. Even if he was the one who desired divorce, his former wife's remarriage to you can bring all of his emotions, regrets, anger, or pain to the surface. Around the wedding, a distant father may become heavily involved, and a cordial dad may become challenging (see the Active-Duty Dad below). To try and head this off at the pass, begin communicating the No-Threat Message as soon as marriage seems certain.

place, consider giving him the following message. If you have a very cooperative relationship with your ex-husband-in-law, this might not be necessary (as his threat level is already low), but if not, take it under advisement.

"Why shouldn't I be concerned? He gets more time with my kids than I do." I had invited Steve to a consultation and had asked him about his relationship with his ex-wife's new husband. Steve's four children lived with their mother, Lauren, and their stepdad, Jason. I had been asked by Jason to counsel the family and try to help them move up Stepdad Mountain. After a few meetings with various family members, it became clear to me that although Steve was not overtly working to sabotage Jason's relationships with his kids, he sure didn't mind tossing a few verbal sticks and stones at Jason every once in a while. "So you're worried that Jason's time with your kids, given that they are at his house much more than they are at yours, will steal them away from you. Is that right?" I asked. "I don't know that I would say 'steal' . . . but yes, I don't want him thinking he can just move in and take over."

Steve is afraid. At the heart of his negative comments is the fear of losing his place in their lives. The No-Threat Message tries to settle those fears by clearly articulating respect to the dad and your agenda in relation to his kids.

Face-to-face verbal communication (man to man) is the best-case scenario, but for the stepdad coping with a tenuous or hostile environment, the message can be communicated by phone, email, or letter.

> Ed, since I am involved with your kids, I wanted to take a minute to
> communicate with you. I want to share that I totally understand and
> respect that you are the only father of these children. I'm not their dad and
> I will never try to take your place. They are your children. I am honored
> to be an added parent figure in their lives. Like a coach, I view my role as
> one of support to their mom and you. My hope is to be a blessing to them.
> I promise to speak well of you and work together for their benefit. Please
> know that I pray for you and for them. If there's anything I can do to help
> or if you have any questions, please contact me.

Feel free to use your own words, but do you hear the spirit of
the message? "I am not a threat to you." That's what he needs to
hear . . . and see. Be sure to back up these words with actions. Give
him the special seat at the parent-teacher meeting, encourage the
kids to enjoy their time with him, take the backseat every once in a
while so he gets extra time with them, and respect his boundaries
and preferences for the children when you can (as long as it's not
a moral issue). Doing so will reinforce that you are not a threat to
his role in the family.

Children need to hear this, too. Just the other day an eleven-
year-old sat in my office and made it clear that her stepdad was not
her dad. "I like Jared, just as long as he doesn't try to take my dad's
place or anything." Children often set their jaw against a stepdad who
seems to be moving in on the special place in their heart reserved
just for Dad. That's why they can relax around you when you make
it clear that you aren't trying to do any such thing.

TYPES OF BIOLOGICAL DADS

Not all ex-husbands-in-law are the same, and they don't all stay
the same, either. This section will review some types of ex-husbands-
in-law. Be sure to read them all, as yours may shift in and out of
roles over time (and it's common for more than one descriptor to
fit the same man). Deceased fathers live on in the memories of their

children and former wife; therefore, go ahead and give consideration to these categories if your wife was widowed.

As you read these descriptions, keep in mind that what is most important in dealing with your ex-husband-in-law is not what kind of person he is, but what kind of person you are. In all things, walk with integrity, humility, and mutual respect as you seek to live at peace.

The Engaged, Open Dad

This is the dad who makes your life easier. He is actively engaged in the training and encouragement of his children and, because he is secure within himself, he is not intimidated or threatened by you. This leaves him open to your presence, reasonable in negotiation, and considerate of your wife's relationship with their children. This dad might even pray that you be a positive role model for his children, that they respect you and perhaps even love you. I know, I know . . . sounds pie in the sky, doesn't it? But it does happen. If this is your ex-husband-in-law, count your blessings, for they are many.

By the way, the Engaged, Open Dad practices good fathering. That is, he practices at being a good father and knows what a good father is. You might learn from his example—and if you have children of your own, you'll want to be one yourself!

> ### Stepdad to Stepdad
>
> "My ex-husband-in-law is a good Christian man, a very good father, and has always treated me well. I think one of the mistakes I made early on was not meeting with him regularly and seeking his help with his daughter. He might have been able to better help her deal with her loyalty issues and the ugliness that stemmed from that. He might have been an asset for me."
>
> Andy

In his excellent manual on fathering, *The 7 Secrets of Effective Fathers,* my friend Dr. Ken Canfield describes the qualities of extraordinary dads. According to Dr. Canfield's research, engaged fathers are committed to their children. They spend more time with their children than ordinary fathers, think about how to nurture their children, and are committed to maintaining their influence in the child's life over time. They also know their child's needs, temperament,

Adult Stepchildren

These descriptions can also apply to biological dads with grown children.

and daily activities. They strive to be involved with their child in many contexts like school, home, and in the community. They also know something about child development (what to expect from children at given ages) and how their children compare to their peers. This knowledge helps them engage the child in appropriate ways. Other qualities include:

- responding consistently to the child over time in mood, morality, ethics, and interests

- protecting children by taking leadership within the home (especially at a time of crisis)

- providing a steady, reliable income for material needs

- providing children with a healthy model for masculine behavior toward a woman

- having good communication skills

- providing spiritual direction in the home[3]

From one father to another, I must confess that I find the above description a bit overwhelming. So I choose to think of it as a treasure map that I can follow, one that brings great reward to everyone in my home. Perhaps you can, too.

The Trying Dad

This father is trying the best he can to be a good parent. He might not have a lot of skills or be as responsible as everyone wishes, but he is trying. Sometimes stepdads will get along nicely with this man; other times you don't see eye to eye and it brings tension. He might say you are a decent guy, but that doesn't mean he won't be a little sarcastic about you at times, as well.

Getting along with this dad is about finding the balance. For instance, having polite, casual conversation at a school event or piano recital goes a long way to keeping cordial feelings between homes. Staying out of a tiff between your wife and him does, too. I asked a group of stepdads what suggestions they would have for managing relationships with an ex-husband-in-law, and this is what rose to the top. These will likely be helpful with the Trying Dad:

- Make good, direct communication your rule of thumb. Don't use the kids as a conduit.

- When being dispassionate is called for, use email or texting.

- Send status updates on the kids whether asked for or not. This communicates consideration for his feelings and his desire to know how they are doing.

- Don't stoop to his level. If he becomes disrespectful or disagreeable, manage yourself and don't reciprocate. It always makes you look worse than him.

- Don't be afraid to ask for help. Asking the dad for his opinion on how to deal with his children shows respect and might earn you some respect. Asking for help might complicate things, but it's worth a try.

The Disengaged or Deactivated Dad

Unfortunately, some dads disengage from the process of parenting while others deactivate altogether. Sometimes fathers disengage because they are puzzled by child rearing and child development and just aren't sure what to do. Even though they love their children immensely, they run from "not knowing" to the safety of emotional distance. These fathers would benefit greatly from taking a class or reading Dr. Canfield's book on parenting. Other Disengaged Dads are paralyzed by emotional exhaustion, fear, or guilt. The fear of losing their children to their mother or guilt over what the kids have suffered can make a dad back away from active parenting. Withdrawing for a season is one thing, but completely deactivating is another.

Fatherlessness is a major issue in America today, and divorce makes it worse. One classic nationally representative study found that less than half of children age eleven to seventeen years with divorced parents had seen their fathers *the previous year* and almost 40 percent had no contact with their fathers *in five years*.[4] There are multiple reasons why this might be, but an all-too-common one is a Deactivated Dad who stops pursuing his children after the divorce. Even men who had been very active fathers sometimes drop out of their children's lives after the family breakup. Dr. James Bray, who studied a group of stepfamilies for over a decade, found that 10 to 15 percent of nonresidential fathers vanished from their kids' lives. These Suddenly Vanishing Fathers, as he called them, were often avoiding the pain associated with their divorce by emotionally disconnecting from their kids and ex-wife.[5]

The Deactivated Dad may be trying to cope with his pain (or displacing the guilt he feels for not being with his kids), but he is creating pain for his children. If this is the scenario for your stepchildren, pray for them diligently; it is a dreadful situation. The challenge for you is to keep a respectful tone when talking about him or dealing with him. When the blind attachment-based loyalties of your stepchildren lead them to speak favorably about

> **Stepdad Wisdom**
>
> "I tried early on to work with him and to offer compromises when the children had scheduled events or activities on his weekends, but he would never cooperate. This resulted in resentment by his children for having to miss something that was important to them. Even when it was within his power to take them to an event or function, he wouldn't do so. I decided that the best course of action was to cease all interaction with him unless it came to defending my wife or advocating for the boys."
>
> Jack

him (even though he has disappointed them repeatedly), you may be tempted to set the record straight. Be very cautious about doing so. Trying to change a child's fantasy of their father often bounces animosity back at you. Similarly, when interacting with a Deactivated Dad (or a Disengaged Dad), you may be tempted to challenge him to reengage. Step carefully. While your intentions are on target, you are unlikely to make progress.

So what should you do in these situations? Look for opportunities to discuss what the child or dad is saying or doing, but do not become emotionally invested in the outcome. For example, with a child who is crediting their father with being responsible when he isn't, engage the conversation gently. "I can tell you are certain your dad will show up as promised this weekend. [Shift the focus to the child, not the dad.] You really are hoping to see him, aren't you? I hope you get to. You are a great kid and deserve to spend some time with him." Again, the trick is not getting caught in the trap of trying to change the child's belief about his or her father. You don't have enough influence to make that happen; unfortunately, that is something the child has to teach himself (and it will be a sad day when he does). Instead, focus on your relationship with the child (not their relationship with their dad), and affirm them. Moving toward the child's heart is what will give you influence—and make you a source of comfort when the reality of their dad's deactivation sets in—over time.

> ### Step-Money
>
> It is tempting to pursue back child support from a disengaged dad to punish his bad behavior or to try and activate him. Neither is a good reason. Taking legal measures to pursue back child support should be about the children's needs only—not yours. Choose your battles wisely.

Terminating Parental Rights. In extreme situations, a Deactivated Dad might be so removed that he gives up his parental rights or finds them legally terminated by the courts because of physical or sexual abuse or psychiatric problems. Children in such circumstances sometimes agree to the termination and may or may not then give the stepfather their blessing to adopt them (which you may or may not choose to do).[6]

When children are ambivalent about legally terminating their father's rights, both you and your wife should be very cautious about pushing them in that direction. Again, trying to change the relationship between your stepchildren and their father is a huge path to family stress and self-sabotage. Follow the child's lead; it is their relationship to manage.

Separate from that important factor, here is another consideration in deciding whether to adopt your stepchildren: Think of adoption as the capstone to your relationship with the children, not a path to it. If you have already built a solid relationship of love and trust and the biological father's rights have been terminated, then adoption will simply be a formality honoring what is. People, however, who think of adoption as the path to greater trust and closeness may be setting everyone up for disappointment. Move forward very cautiously.

The Active-Duty Dad

On the surface, the Active-Duty Dad appears to be an Engaged Dad. He is supportive, present, and interested in his children's lives. But there is a key difference. He is motivated not with self-confidence and a pure passion for his kids, but with fear. His activation is duty driven by the fear that if he doesn't engage, he might lose his kids. There are two types of Active-Duty Dads reacting to two types of crises: The Divorce-Activated Dad and the Remarriage-Activated Dad.[7]

Sometimes divorce is a wake-up call that results in positive growth for a father; the divorce activation in his life is a blessing for his kids. But other Divorce-Activated Dads are just reacting in fear to the possibility of losing their kids. In effect, parenting is another field of play for the power game between them and their ex-wife.

Similarly, Remarriage-Activated Dads are selfishly trying to protect their turf. "He is jealous and upset at the prospect of another man—a stepfather—supplanting him in his children's lives. He is their father, and he does not want another man stealing that role away from him."[8] This man is competitive and you are the competition.

Sometimes the Remarriage-Activated Dad blindsides his ex-wife because her co-parenting history with him misleads Mom to believe that he won't be an issue in her new marriage. During courtship, you may have even thought you benefitted from his emotional distance. But marriage often changes things (lots of things!). Once it's clear that you aren't going away anytime soon, the remarriage activates his presence. You might have been able to pretend that you had "blended" as a family before, but not anymore. In addition, unresolved issues from your wife's previous marriage to him—issues that had long been lying dormant—can be resurrected upon his activation. All of a sudden your wife finds herself fussing and feuding with him in the same way that they did before the divorce.

Obviously, either the Divorce- or Remarriage-Activated Dad is a challenge for you because he is defensive and easily threatened. So what can you do?

- The No-Threat Message will likely fall on deaf ears because this dad's fear and insecurity are immense. But it's still worth a shot; what do you have to lose?

- Resist the temptation to stand as protector against his controlling behavior. Ironically, the best way for you to defend your wife is to encourage her to deal with him directly. Spend time talking about how she can respond and help her develop a game plan, but let her take the lead. Unless there is significant reason your wife can't do it, you need to play second violin in this situation, too.

- Your stepchildren probably won't discern their dad's motivations; they don't care, they just enjoy having him around. So try to encourage and celebrate their time with him and again resist the urge to set the record straight.

Finally, a gut check for those of you with kids of your own: are you a Disengaged, Deactivated, or Divorce/Remarriage-Activated Dad? Perhaps you wrestle with guilt over not being available to your children (drawing close to your stepchildren can make that feeling more intense). Or perhaps you feel disloyal, finding it hard, for example, to really enjoy your stepchildren because you know your kids feel cheated of their time with you. If so, begin your journey toward pure motivations and the freedom to love by acknowledging your intense emotions. You must be honest with yourself so that your actions won't be dictated by your fear, guilt, or hurt. Next, if you need to reconcile a relationship with one of your children, talk to your wife and start working on it now. You and your children won't be able to find forgiveness or freedom in your current family situations until you reconnect. By the way, many conflictual stepdad-stepchild relationships are improved when the stepdad finds peace with his own children. And finally, while working on reconciling your relationships, humbly acknowledge to your stepchildren how your feelings have contributed to any distance or difficulties between you. That act of humility might soften the discord and give both of you a second chance.

The Angry or Addicted Dad

This dad is chaos waiting to happen. He may float in and out of the children's lives with renewed commitment only to vanish again for his favorite drink, drug, or latest obsession. He is irresponsible and undependable; instability is his middle name. When anger is part of the dynamic, it might even be hidden in religiosity.

"He is still a hostile jerk," Tim began about his wife's ex. "He destroyed two marriages, and his four older children want nothing to do with him. Our oldest son recently stopped visiting him, and it is only a matter of time before the twelve-year-old stops, too. He calls himself a Christian. He knows Scripture very well, but he uses it to bludgeon people into submitting to his will; he is a religious Pharisee. His continual attacks, calling my wife and me adulterers because we remarried (there was no adultery), liars because we disagree with his views on Scripture, and thieves because he pays child support, certainly make for a very difficult dynamic. We do our best not to speak ill of him and even find that we must stop the boys from ridiculing their father. It is a very difficult situation."

This dad presents a huge challenge. He poses a constant threat to the stability of your home. His children resent him one day and miss him the next. And although he repeatedly hurts them, their fierce loyalty keeps them longing for his return. The resulting ambiguity keeps everyone, especially you, searching for solid ground. Surviving in this situation requires learning to live with a lack of predictability or control and gaining tolerance for the vacillating closeness and distance mechanisms in your stepchildren. Unfortunately, their openness to you is often a direct reflection of his movement in and out of their lives.

These circumstances also demand strong communication with your wife, who is also often overwhelmed and defeated by her ex-husband's chaos. If he speaks harshly or angrily to her, the protective side of you will naturally want to stand up for her and perhaps fight her battles—any man can turn into the Incredible Hulk if his wife is being threatened! But it may not be best for you to do so. To be clear, I'm not speaking so much here of his being physically intimidating or abusive (if he becomes so, feel free to turn green), but more of times when he hurts her feelings. Haphazardly jumping in to take over, even with the best intentions, may backfire.

A couple approached me at a conference one weekend with this very issue. Her ex-husband would belittle her (just as he had done during their marriage) when discussing co-parenting matters. The stepdad had been quick to defend her and had inadvertently escalated the negativity between homes. His wife was very resentful—appreciative, yes—but also resentful. Part of the problem was that his wife didn't know why he was doing this. I suggested he pull back from being the white knight and give attention to communicating clearly with his wife about his feelings of anger and concern for her and then dialogue with her about how he could be helpful. What develops at that point will be a tailored prescription suitable to the couple. And, of course, that's the point: negotiating a solution that keeps you connected as a couple.

> **For Mom**
>
> What type of dad is the father of your children? Share your insights with your husband and discuss the implications for co-parenting and between-home cooperation.

Without question, the Angry or Addicted Dad is destructive and difficult to deal with. So how else do you cope?

DEALING WITH A DESTRUCTIVE DAD

This portion of Stepdad Mountain is often extremely taxing. Actually, I should clarify the word *portion*. It's not a section of the climb that you conquer once and move on with it behind you. In reality, if you are dealing with any of the above difficult ex-husbands-in-law, you know that this portion of the climb is cyclical, ever before you. The intensity of the conflict may subside from time to time, but until there is significant growth and change in his heart and life, his weight will add burden to your climb.

In our book *The Smart Stepmom,* my coauthor Laura Petherbridge had some encouraging words for stepmoms dealing with similar circumstances.

> Philippians 2:5 tells us that the Holy Spirit is willing and capable to give us the mind of Christ: "Let this mind be in you, which was also in Christ Jesus" (KJV). That means we now have the ability to think and act like Jesus. I can't speak for you, but for me this is incredibly good news. Because left to my own thoughts and actions, I can be nasty—in particular if I'm being slandered, criticized, or ridiculed. . . . But God's Word tells me there is a better way to respond, a method that can motivate peace rather than destruction.[9]

I offer those same words of encouragement for you here.

In addition, God gives us specific instructions in the latter half of Romans 12 on how to respond to an unreasonable person.[10] There Paul outlines the attitudes and actions needed in order to love difficult people. God's prescription for overcoming an evil person is to respond with good. The temptation we all face is to repay evil with more evil. But that is not in keeping with the mercies God has shown us (Romans 12:1). The goal, in spite of the hurt we experience at the hands of others, is to offer ourselves as living sacrifices and repay evil with good. But what about revenge? Isn't that justified?

Vengeance, according to our Lord, is not ours to take. Romans 12:19 makes it clear that God is the only one who should seek vengeance. He is the only one who is pure and holy, with no ulterior motives. He always desires our higher good (even when we don't deserve it). If your wife's former husband chooses to continue with evil, destructive deeds instead of good, it is God's job to do what is best. Not yours.

But what is your role in the meantime? Are you supposed to sit around and passively wait for more persecution? No, the answer is to become aggressive with good. When wicked behavior is running rampant, it seems to have control. However, God's Word tells us that good is more powerful than evil. God does not say that doing good to others will help us tolerate their evil. He says that we can *overcome* it. Light overwhelms darkness. Hope triumphs over discouragement. Love casts out fear. It is our task, in the face of evil, to offer good. Why? Because good invites repentance. Consider Romans 12:20: "If your enemy is hungry, feed him; if he is thirsty, give him something to drink. In doing this, you will heap burning coals on his head." The phrase "heap burning coals on his head" refers to awakening the conscience of another. With good, we can melt the heart of evil with burning shame. Constantly repaying evil with good holds a mirror up to the perpetrator reflecting their evil; in some cases this will bring about a change of heart.

But what if repentance does not happen in the heart of the destructive dad? Then it's between your ex-husband-in-law and his Creator. You may suffer much at his hand, but you must trust God to do what is right. And what do you get for your obedience? Another place in Scripture concludes that the Lord will reward those who do good to those who are evil (Proverbs 25:22). The evil of some ex-husbands-in-law can be overcome, others cannot. Either way, the Lord will notice your sacrifice and reward you.

Until then, live this way (see Romans 12:14–20):

- Bless and do not curse.

- Do everything you can to live in harmony.

- Do not be proud; be willing to associate with him despite his behavior.

- Do not become conceited.

- Be careful to do what is right.

- Do not take revenge.

- "Feed him" and "give him something to drink" even when undeserved.

HEROES BY CHOICE

For Group Discussion

1. What frustrations have you had with your ex-husband-in-law?

2. Discuss this statement: "Of course, conflict is a two-way street and you can't control how your ex-husband-in-law behaves, but 'as far as it depends on you, live at peace'" (Romans 12:18).

3. What is the point of the No-Threat Message?

4. What type of dad is your ex-husband-in-law?

   The Open, Engaged Dad
   The Trying Dad
   The Disengaged or Deactivated Dad
   The Active-Duty Dad
   The Angry or Addicted Dad

5. What tips or insights did you discover in the chapter to help you cope with your ex-husband-in-law?

6. Romans 12 reminds us that vengeance belongs to the Lord. What, then, is our role in dealing with difficult people?

7. Review the qualities of effective fathers mentioned on pages 140–141. What can you do to move toward being this type of father and stepfather?

Chapter 9

Your Kids:
What Do They Need?

I've felt extremely pulled to choose between my wife
and my kids. I regret that very much.

ANDY

What my kids have needed most
from me is stability and the
assurance that I will never leave
them like their mother did.

JERRY

"Please tell your husband I sympathize with his struggles in your family. I can't imagine how frustrating it must be to be him." I was talking with Juanita, a remarried mother of three, and hoping to eventually communicate with her husband, Henry. The couple had been married about four years when Juanita and her

No Children of Your Own?

Two-thirds of stepparents also have biological children of their own. But even if you don't, I recommend you read this chapter. You will receive insight into the emotional dilemmas your wife faces while parenting her children. Balancing parental responsibilities and spousal commitments can be challenging. Read this chapter with an eye for how it applies to your home.

three children came to therapy. She had invited her husband, but so far he wouldn't attend.

"I think he's afraid of being blamed for all that's going on," she theorized, "but I know it's not all his fault. All of us share the blame." She was right. There was enough responsibility to go around: Her children had banned together to keep Henry marginalized; Juanita felt caught between her kids and her husband; and her ex-husband moved across the country and was terribly inconsistent as a father. And then there was Henry's part. Though I had never met him, stories shared by Juanita and her children made me wonder if he wasn't feeling like a powerless outsider in his own home and a frustrated father (of his children). He was stuck trying to be a good dad and stepdad with a wife and ex-wife who wouldn't allow him much influence. He was falling down everywhere he stepped.

A TOUGH BALANCING ACT

When you have children of your own, the Smart Stepdad balancing act is even more difficult. Instead of juggling three objects (as if that's not hard enough), you're tossing around five or more. You add in things like how your stepchildren and children are getting along and the guilt of not being available to your kids as much as you'd like.

But having your own children can also work to your advantage. Being a dad yourself tends to help you sympathize and get along with your ex-husband-in-law; after all, you know something of what he's going through. And some studies suggest that having their own children helps stepdads to be closer to their stepchildren and have more positive feelings toward them[1] (in

> ### For Mom
>
> Read this chapter to understand more of your husband's balancing act. Being dad and stepdad is often confusing and guilt producing. Consider reading *The Smart Stepmom* to help you partner with him to raise his children.

part because your kids have already taught you that even great kids can have sour attitudes sometimes).

Whether for the good or the not-so good, there's no doubt that having your own kids adds complexity to your life. But compared to moms who become stepmoms, dads who become stepdads have an easier time maintaining positive relationships with their children. If your ex-wife has remarried, you may be pleasantly surprised to learn that it's easier for children to have a positive relationship with a nonresidential dad when their mother has remarried than when she is still single.[2]

This is a bit more complicated if your kids' primary residence is with you. When residential single fathers marry and a stepmom takes over many of the daily caretaking responsibilities formerly performed by the father, the change is a more dramatic one for the children and more difficult to adapt to. Even then, though, once the stepfamily has stabilized, resident father-child relationships are often similar to father-child relationships in biological two-parent homes.[3] In other words, being Daddy to your children is very possible, but never take it for granted.

MINISTERING TO YOUR CHILD'S HEART

You may not be a paid minister, but if you are a parent, you are called upon to minister to your child's heart. Essentially our work as parents is teaching, training, and equipping our children for life—this life and the one beyond. The loss (i.e., death or divorce) that brought you and your children to your current family situation demands a special dose of ministry from you. The first part of this chapter outlines general ministry strategies that most dads/stepdads will need to implement, and the second half deals with a few specific dilemmas for some dads/stepdads.

Stay Physically Connected and Emotionally Engaged

Your children need your continued presence in their lives. Remember the chapter 8 discussion of ex-husbands-in-law and how some dads vanish from their children's lives following a divorce or after the mother remarries? You cannot afford to be that dad. Countless books have been written on the critical role of a father—and they are right. No matter what society or the "dumb fathers" of TV sitcoms communicate about fatherhood, you are vitally important to the emotional, psychological, relational, and spiritual development of your children. Even if circumstances or distant living arrangements make your engagement infrequent or difficult, never stop pursuing your kids. (If you are being blocked from involvement, see the section on Daddy Dilemmas at the end of this chapter.) Your kids are better off with an engaged, active father. And so is your stepfamily.

1. Strike a balance in your roles. Think about it. How can your children celebrate your role as a stepfather if it means losing you to their stepsiblings? Watching you abandon ship only to invest in your stepchildren would cause them to think of their stepsiblings and stepmother as the enemy. This competitive environment would certainly sabotage household harmony and cause many conflicts. What is needed is balance between the roles of father and stepdad, not an over-investment in either.

No, you probably won't be able to give equal time to each, but you can strive to be fully present with whomever you are with. Use modern technology (e.g., email and texting) to keep in touch even when you can't be physically present, and seek to play all the roles a father plays, even when at a distance. For example, some dads are tempted not to engage in stern talk or boundary setting with their kids when they don't get to see them much. But your children still need to know you approve of wise choices and disapprove of poor ones. Don't ditch your disciplinarian role just because time is limited.

Striking a balance also means managing your guilt when circumstances give you more time with your stepchildren than with your biological children. Some men try to solve their internal guilt by remaining distant or critical of their stepchildren. But this won't improve your relationship—or your conscience—with your biological children. Researcher James Bray notes, "The man who complains about the sloppy state of his stepchild's room or the child's awful taste in music is really complaining about something else: the loss of his own biological children and how much pain that causes him."[4] This is similar to the loyalty conflicts some stepchildren feel over calling their stepdad Dad. Liking you presents a problem. The answer for them is not in being angry or distant from you. Nor is your solution to displace your guilt on your stepchildren. If you find yourself struggling with this dilemma, try to think of relationships with your children and stepchildren independent of each other and give yourself permission to fully engage in each as you are able. You have enough love to go around.

> ## Stepdad to Stepdad
>
> "Resist playing favorites with your kids. When with my stepchildren, my attention easily switched to my kids. It's natural to do this, but I had to be intentional—I had to pace myself and balance my attention. My stepchildren are now in their twenties and it has paid off."
>
> Gil, stepdad

2. Communicate commitment to your kids while also making it clear that your marriage is a priority. It serves no one's best interests to make an either/or choice between your marriage and your children. Instead, make a both/and decision. Be committed to both your children *and* your marriage. I know this sounds good in theory, but the truth is, living it out is challenging, especially when a child throws a major guilt trip at you: "Do you love your wife more than me?" This either/or choice feels like a no-win situation for you. Recognize it as a both/and dilemma. Your answer needs to reflect a deep love for *both* your children *and* your wife. You might communicate it this way:

Please know that I love you with all my heart. I can see from the way you've been acting lately that you wonder if I still love you as much as I did. You need to know that my marriage and becoming a stepdad has not changed my love for you. I know I'm not as available as I used to be, and we have less time together, but you are still my child and nothing will change that. Yet you need to know that I am choosing to love my wife and stepchildren, too. It's not a competition; God has given me more than enough love for you and them. I love them differently than you, but I do love them. Know this: I will never stop loving you even while I love my wife and will always be her husband, till death do us part. I am hers and she is mine, for life.

Smart Dating

A word of caution: If you are not ready to fully commit yourself to your wife and risk making your children uncomfortable, I strongly urge you to refrain from marriage until you are ready. Resist the temptation to believe that there will never be tension between these two "firsts."

From time to time, children who have experienced tremendous loss and instability in life need to hear in no uncertain terms that you will never stop loving them. We all know that God loves us unconditionally, and yet we all still need to hear the words of the Lord found in Hebrews 13:5, "Never will I leave you; never will I forsake you." The permanence of love brings calm in the storm and peace in the darkness. Flood your children with it. They also need to hear that your marriage is a lifelong, never-say-die, permanent commitment that is second only to your love for the Lord. Over time, those two messages reinforced by your consistent, loving actions will keep your children from getting lost in the shuffle.

3. **Stay predictable in your availability and activities.** Of course, some change before and after marriage is inevitable. But as much as it is within your power, remain consistent in your visitation schedule, phone calls, and pattern of involvement. Doing so builds bridges of trust and encourages your children to be open with you. They need to know that you still care to hear about their daily lives and their thoughts, concerns, and feelings.

4. Compartmentalize special time. From time to time, make opportunities for exclusive time with each of your children. Take your daughter to lunch or your son to a baseball game. Planning special time with individual children happens regularly in biological families and no one thinks anything of it (when balanced between all the children over time). But for some reason, people get paranoid about doing so in stepfamilies. Your wife might object to you taking your daughter to a special concert without taking all of her children, as well, or your ex-wife might accuse you of favoritism for not including all the kids in an activity. But special time helps to feed a child's heart, and as long as everyone gets included over time, it doesn't have to add up to favoritism. Find a balance; have entire family activities where everyone is included, and enjoy individual special events meant to communicate ongoing dedication to your children.

5. Don't buy the lie. I said it before, but it deserves restating: Don't ever be fooled into believing that cutting yourself out of your child's life is to their advantage. Nothing could be further from the truth. "It just seems that my kids' lives would be less complicated if they didn't have to travel to see me every month," Dan explained to me. "Aren't I making life easier for them by letting them stay at their mom's house?" It is true that visitation causes inconveniences for children (and adults), but the blessings far outweigh the difficulties. Don't buy the lie.

> ### Stepdad to Stepdad
>
> "The number one thing my kids needed and still need to know every day is that I'll never leave them as long as God wants me on this earth, and that they'll always have my attention when dealing with any issue they come across. Without question, stability is key."
>
> Thomas

Be Fair and Consistent in Parenting Your Kids

This principle is stated simply enough. But here's the rub: Being respectful of your limited authority with your stepchildren may give the appearance of unfairness and inconsistency to your children.

Francis put it this way: "With biological kids, you are not limited in your role, but with stepkids you are because you are not the lead parent. I struggle to be fair in these situations, but letting my wife take the lead with my stepkids makes my kids question why I'm unfair." Here are a few suggestions.

1. Explain the limitations of your stepdad role. For example, when referencing behavior of your stepchild that your son or daughter witnessed, say, "You and I both know that I would not let you get away with speaking to me that way. But I'm not Karen's father, and this needs to be handled by her mother just like when I let our neighbors punish their own kids. As for you, however, you may not talk to me or your stepmother in that tone." Some people think that saying this out loud is revealing a big secret or something, as if the child doesn't already know. But it's just being honest. The trick is to not criticize your wife for her values or how she is handling the situation. The point is, clearly define yourself as your children's father and, therefore, capable of managing them as you see fit even if it's different from how you manage your stepchildren.

2. Remain consistent with your pre-marriage rules and expectations. Things will change and parenting evolves as we and our children grow, but try to avoid dramatic changes to rules if possible. Unless, of course, before becoming a stepdad you were inconsistent and undisciplined as a father. Giving yourself a pass because you were permissive isn't helpful to anyone. Talk with your wife and try to set mutual expectations for the home and raise the expectations for your children (see chapters 5 to 7). This will come with a price tag (resistance and objections from your kids), but better now than later.

Don't Push Your Children Into Steprelationships

In my first book *The Smart Stepfamily: Seven Steps to a Healthy Family*, I suggested that stepfamilies should not be combined in a blender. Trying to force relationships between the ingredients of your family just creates stress and expectations of love or affection that can't be demanded. Instead I suggested cooking your stepfamily slowly and with much patience, as in a Crockpot. Charles and his wife, Debra, caught the wisdom of this approach and stuck to it. After a few years, he wrote me with reflections of how his children, stepchildren, and wife formed their relationships.

> When my kids came to visit for the weekend, they would hug some and shake hands with others, but after a while, her kids would migrate back to her and mine to me. At first we thought we had to group everyone together all the time so they would like each other. But we learned that it was okay to let them go where it was safe. We let them have their own space and do their own thing, and respected when and how they chose to come together. Things got better when we relaxed and didn't throw on the blender switch. We let them simmer and come together with a long, moderate heat.

Let your kids work out their degree of openness to and fondness for their stepmom and stepsiblings in their own time. But balance this with sources of low heat for the family Crockpot: Encourage shared activities when it is of natural interest to everyone involved, and create a climate that fosters relationship development. For example, expect basic respect and courteous behavior toward one another. Until children trust that others respect their personal space and property, they won't care to deepen their relationships with one another. And finally, be sure to give your children permission to love and remain loyal to their biological mother (see chapter 4). The paradox is this: If you insist they love their stepmom, you may inadvertently embolden their loyalty to their mother, but if you insist on mother respect and make love for their stepmom their choice, they may feel freer to gravitate toward your wife. (To be clear, respectful and courteous behavior toward your wife is not optional, but love and feelings of affection are.) The difference is freedom. When love is demanded, it becomes more difficult to obtain. But when love is a free choice, it can be discovered sooner.

Help Maintain Social Connections

Another way to minister to your child's heart throughout the transition to a healthy stepfamily is to make decisions that maintain your child's social network and connections. This is especially true for preteen and adolescent-aged children. Within a year of the death of our middle son, Connor, my wife and I were faced with some career decisions that would have meant moving our family. Our oldest son was fifteen at that time and had some healthy school and youth-group friendships that we saw as an asset for him. Our life had been traumatized enough; throwing one more unwanted transition his direction would not have been wise. So we passed on the opportunity—and I don't regret it a bit. If at all possible, don't let your role as stepdad force your kids into an unwanted move away from family, friends, or a church community that is serving their needs.

> ### Adult Children
>
> Don't underestimate how left out adult children sometimes feel. They may feel jealous, for example, of the time you spend with stepfamily members. Maintain connections (e.g., regular phone calls, monthly lunch dates, and annual Christmas celebrations) with them and your grandchildren. When both her children and your children are together, be sure to balance your attention. Focusing too much energy on your stepkids can be a mistake.

Advocate for Your Kids When Necessary

God intended for parenting to be a two-person job. It's good to share the weight of responsibility with someone else; I think we make better decisions that way. Another advantage is that each parent gets to help the other be a better parent. My wife has coached me many times and I her. Sometimes we reflect observations to the other ("I'm not sure you realize how angry you were"); other times perspective ("Just because a male is silent for a while doesn't mean anything is wrong"). Over time, we help each other to be better parents.

You and your wife can and should do the same. One added complication to be aware of, however, is how easy it is to become defensive about your own children. Guard against this, for it closes you off to how the other is trying to help. But what do you do if you don't care for how she managed a situation? How do you approach her without igniting her defenses?

Humility is a good start. You might try saying something like, "Sweetheart, I'd like to talk with you about what happened last night when I was out of the house. I know in the past I've been pretty defensive about my kids and made you feel small compared to them. I regret that very much and am trying hard not to do that now. Having said that, can I share some things with you that I think will help both you and them? [Get confirmation of her readiness to hear you.] I'm concerned that the way you respond in X situation is coming across as mean or uncaring to the kids and it's putting a bigger wedge between you. I know you don't want that, and neither do I. I know you are trying to teach the kids responsibility—and I love you for that. I'm wondering if we can talk about how to go about handling this in the future so they get the responsibility message. Knowing my kids, perhaps you could respond this way . . ."

Hopefully this will lower everyone's defensives and open the door to cooperation. Negotiating a set of parental responses on which you agree is important. If repeated discussions do not result in agreement, take the matter outside your marriage. Attend a class together or seek counsel from a parent educator or therapist so you can develop a shared system of parenting. Most important, don't turn the discussion into a you-versus-us battle or everyone loses.

DADDY DILEMMAS

Let's turn our attention to some specific dilemmas that not all dads/stepdads face, but many do.

If You Are Blocked From Your Kids

Earlier I emphasized remaining connected and involved with your kids. This is a frustrating prescription for some dads because they are trying but find themselves blocked by their ex-wife, extended family members, or the kids themselves. Or perhaps you are currently disconnected from your kids because of your own choices and don't know how to reconnect. In either case, realize that you are still important to your kids (even if it isn't apparent), and that the father-child bond is not easily broken. All is not lost.

Try to reconnect at every opportunity. Many men just give up (the rejection is less intense), but that sends the wrong message to your children. Even if they don't seem to reciprocate your efforts, you want them waking up in five years knowing that you pursued them continuously.

If you are disconnected as a result of your own choices, try to reconnect, but be very patient. Their hurt may cause them to be unresponsive at first.

Opening Shut Doors

If you've been disconnected, getting your kids to open up can be difficult sometimes. Try these tips:

- Listen first, ask questions, then begin talking about what's on your mind.
- Let them settle in to your house by doing something they enjoy first; then invite them to get a Coke or play a game.
- Be sure your home includes games, activities, etc., that they enjoy. Engage with them.
- Listening to music is a good way to open the heart.

Matt Crain, PhD, *ConnectingFathers.com*

If blocked by others, take advantage of any avenue, however small. For example, communicate messages through an extended family member or use technology to share your heart with your child. One father I know wrote letters to his kids that he knew they would never receive. He kept copies of the letters just in case life reopened the door to their relationship. After ten years of alienation, his children were old enough to pursue a relationship with him on their own. He shared the letters with them and they were able to catch up on his love and thoughts for them over the years. Plus, it proved that the lies their mother had told them were not representative of his heart. It was a tremendous blessing for this father and his kids.

Being a Nonresident Dad

Eighty percent of nonresident parents are men;[5] their children primarily live elsewhere. Your continued visitation, communication, and contact with nonresidential children is vital. It has a positive effect on your child's emotional and social well-being and helps reduce risky adolescent behavior.[6] In addition, your continued child support is critical to raising your child's standard of living, which in turn is directly related to many matters of child well-being.[7] Most of all, paying child support clearly communicates your continued commitment to your children separate and apart from your relationship with their mother.

Staying in Touch

Here are some tips from Matt Crain, PhD, *ConnectingFathers.com,* for staying in touch with your kids:

- Maintain communication routines. Write a letter/email on Monday morning, call Tuesday evening, send a text message on Thursday, and keep your appointed visitation. Be sure to remember birthdays and holidays with a card, phone call, or something appropriate. Young children will benefit from your recording a bedtime story and making it available on CD.

- Take pictures of the activities you and your child engage in (even routine chores around the house) and be sure they have a copy. This reminds them of your presence and engages the heart even when you can't be physically present.

- Get out of the house. Making the most of your time together often results from getting away from video games, your favorite TV chair, and their being able to "chill" in their bedroom. Walk around the block, explore the backyard, run errands together—whatever it takes.

One often overlooked complication of being a nonresidential father is how it impacts your wife, who becomes a nonresidential stepmother. Due to reduced time with stepkids, nonresidential stepmoms are less likely to take on a parental role and are less close with stepchildren than are residential stepmoms. This, of course, makes sense, because less time in the stepfamily Crockpot means less cooking time. It's just harder for her to find her place with your kids, which adds stress. This stress might then translate into tension with you when your kids come to visit, especially if you indulge their preferences or cater to their desires.

To avoid this pressure, lower your expectations regarding the level of closeness between your wife and kids. Let them work this out in their own time. In anticipation of their visits, talk with your wife about how the weekend will go, listen to her needs, and share yours. This will help to prevent unrealistic expectations from sabotaging your time together.

SURVIVING THE STEPFAMILY FOREST

Therapists and stepfamily educators John and Emily Visher used to joke that stepfamilies don't have a family tree, they have a family forest! As seedlings in the forest, your children can easily get lost among the towering trees and foliage. A little extra water and warm sunshine from you can do wonders.

HEROES BY CHOICE

For Group Discussion

(Stepdads without children are encouraged to participate in this discussion, especially if having your own child is a future possibility.)

1. What challenges have you faced in balancing your roles as dad and stepdad?

2. What guilt feelings have you experienced regarding your children?

3. In what ways are you trying to stay physically connected and emotionally engaged with your kids?

4. How are you trying to fulfill these things?

   - Strike a balance in your roles as father, husband, and stepdad.
   - Communicate commitment to your kids while also making it clear that your marriage is a priority.
   - Stay predictable in your availability and activities.
   - Compartmentalize special time. From time to time, make opportunities for exclusive time with each of your children.
   - Don't buy the lie. Don't be fooled into believing that cutting yourself out of your child's life is to their advantage.

5. What are some strategies for being fair and consistent with rules for your kids?

6. How patient are you in allowing steprelationships to develop between your kids and your wife or stepchildren?

7. How can advocating for your kids be delicate with your wife?

8. If you are blocked from your kids or a nonresident father, review Matt Crain's tips for Opening Shut Doors (p. 164) or Staying in Touch (p. 165). Which are helpful? What have you already found works for you?

Chapter 10

Hugging Your Stepdaughter, Stepsibling Attractions, and the Awkward Issues of Stepfamily Sexuality

It was weird. One minute she was my little princess
and the next a young woman. All of a sudden I was
uncomfortable with her sitting on my lap.

SEAN

Now eighteen, my stepdaughter is very pretty just like
her mom. As she grew up I was amazed at how beautiful
she became, but I never saw her as sexually attractive
nor did I feel awkward hugging her. Actually, her mom
and I worry about how attractive she is to other guys
more than anything else.

BOB

As the resident father figure and masculine role model in your
home, you have the incredible opportunity to demonstrate for your

stepchildren biblical character, humility, and the power of living a Christian life. For example, you can teach your stepson how to stand up for godliness even when his friends don't. The way you treat your stepdaughter, protect her, reinforce her God-given worth, and even how you treat her mother contribute invaluably to her sense of self-esteem and femininity. Hugging your stepdaughter hugs her heart.

HUGGING YOUR STEPDAUGHTER

For Mom

Only 15 percent of mothers talked with their future husband before marriage about the tricky aspects of physical contact with stepdaughters.[1] It is an uncomfortable topic, but don't avoid it. Read this chapter and discuss how it applies to your family situation.

There's another side to this opportunity—a dark side if you will. And for many men, to talk about it is embarrassing. But to fall prey to it would be highly destructive and much worse.

Brent never found himself sexually attracted to his stepdaughter, but he felt self-conscience at times. He found himself cautious about the possibilities of what could happen and guarded against situations that would make his stepdaughter feel uncomfortable. So he paid attention to how he dressed. "Getting married meant I had to change my habit of walking around the house in my underwear or even going without a shirt. And I certainly asked her mom to make sure my stepdaughter dressed appropriately, as well."

Through the years, courageous people have sidelined me at a conference or emailed us at Successful Stepfamilies with desperate questions about sexuality within stepfamilies. Some were guys like Brent who were trying to prevent problems. Others were dealing with situations that had already crossed adult-child boundaries or with the awkward circumstances of stepsiblings who find themselves romantically attracted to one another (more on that later). But no matter the circumstance, they were all trying to correctly handle the situation. I admire that.

What I appreciate about Brent is his nerve to openly admit to the need for high integrity in his home. He could have downplayed the issue and shrugged it off, but he didn't. He courageously admitted that the situation required proactive planning and preventive action on his part. That's to be commended.

Passing Thoughts

But what if you are active in preventing inappropriate behaviors and you still find yourself struggling with unwanted thoughts? You don't have to be a pervert to experience an uncomfortable feeling when giving a hug to your stepdaughter when no one else is in the room, or to have passing sexual thoughts about her. The vast majority of stepdads will never cross the line into entertaining such thoughts or acting on them,* but some will be greatly surprised by an incidental thought, curiosity, or wonderment. Then what do you do?

Sean admitted to some passing sexual attractions to his stepdaughter. I appreciated his honesty because it indicated a desire to keep his thoughts and behaviors in check. "I have found my stepdaughter to be very attractive and I do get uncomfortable hugging her. My worst nightmare is for her to catch me looking at her body or breasts, so I work hard to look her in the eyes. I have had a few fantasy thoughts about her, but not often, and I quickly dismiss them." Sean is aware of his vulnerability and is striving to manage it appropriately. When a stepdad doesn't manage such vulnerabilities, however, lives are ripped apart.

We've all heard news accounts of stepfathers who have been arrested for molesting their stepdaughters (such shocking headlines sell lots of broadcast time and newspapers, so we tend to hear about

---

*Clearly, a man who sexually touches a stepchild is being abusive. This must be reported to the authorities and he must seek treatment. A man who has repetitive sexual thoughts about a child—even if he has not acted on them—should seek psychological treatment as well.

them). Thankfully in our culture there are laws and social pressures against such behaviors because they are so destructive to children (and marriages). A few years ago I was stunned by a phone interview I conducted at the request of a newspaper in Singapore. The interview went as most generally do, but the reporter kept asking me questions about sexuality and the incidence of stepfather molestation. I paused the interview and asked her why she was pressing me on that issue. According to her, the Malaysian culture turned a blind eye to stepfather-stepdaughter sexual touching and even encouraged it on some level. The problem was running rampant and she hoped to offer some perspective through our interview. I was more than willing to oblige her; I spoke in no uncertain terms how damaging such conduct would be to a child and how it sabotaged emotional safety within the home (even if culturally condoned). That interview reminded me to be thankful that we don't have that abhorrent climate in most Western societies. But it still can happen in any given home.

> ### Dating and Part-time Stepdads
>
> A deepening bond with a stepdaughter diminishes sexual attractions; the more fatherly you become toward her, the less sexual confusion there is. That's why dating or part-time stepdads must be on guard. Infrequent or limited time with a stepchild adds vulnerability.

Sean could have had that environment in his home, but he took a few steps to prevent it.

- "I have found my stepdaughter to be attractive." Sean admitted to himself and another person his vulnerability. As embarrassing as it is, submitting himself to accountability takes some power out of this weakness; it sheds light on an otherwise dark secret, which makes acting on it less likely.

- "My worst nightmare . . ." Sean has owned how destructive his potential sin would be for his stepdaughter (and family). Men who fall prey to such temptations often minimize the potential impact of their behavior on others, which allows for a psychological justification of the risks involved. ("It's not a big deal; no one will get hurt.") Make no mistake, inappropriate behavior toward your stepdaughter will have a devastating impact on her emotionally, psychologically, and spiritually, not to mention jeopardize your marriage and subject you to criminal proceedings. It is a nightmare you don't want to become reality.

- "I work hard to look her in the eyes." Like Job, Sean made a covenant with his eyes not to look at a woman—in this case his stepdaughter—lustfully (Job 31:1). This commitment has many applications, but one is to simply bounce your eyes in another direction within a couple seconds of noticing her body or developing sexuality.[2] It takes discipline, but this simple action can help reduce inappropriate thoughts immediately.

- "I quickly dismiss them." Similar to bouncing his eyes in a different direction, Sean bounces inappropriate thoughts and images out of his head. Entertaining sexual thoughts about anyone other than your wife is the beginning of a long road that will not have a good end. You must guard your thoughts to guard your heart (Proverbs 4:23).

Withdrawing to a Safe Distance?

If you have a stepdaughter, the last section probably made you uneasy. Sorry. It wasn't meant to scare you, just to serve as a yellow Caution sign beside the road. But I'd better balance the discussion now or you might be tempted to withdraw to a safe distance.

If there's one predictable pattern in us men it is the tendency to withdraw when we aren't sure of the relationship, when we experience conflict, or when we are fearful of being hurt or causing hurt. When stepdads appropriately withdraw from conveying sexual messages to a stepdaughter, they can inadvertently pull too far, removing their affirmations, as well. That, too, can bring harm if it communicates disaffection, rejection, or disinterest. It's a real Catch-22. So what can you do?

First, realize that harm is in the extremes. Obviously you cross a boundary if you make romantic or sexual advances toward a stepdaughter, but you also deny her healthy affirmation if you with-draw so far that your affections and positive encouragement can't be reached. Seek a balance in your posture.

If you haven't already, seek your wife's input into how you can find the balance. If you're not sure how to bridge into that discussion, use this chapter as an objective catalyst to the conversation. (Mom, if you are reading this, don't be quick to judge him. Help him to be proactive in loving your daughter appropriately.) Together you can discuss the meaning of affection and how it is expressed in your home and extended families in general. Try to match your style to what your stepdaughter will be accustomed and open to.

Stepdad to Stepdad

"With my older stepdaughters I stick to side hugs and fore-head-type kisses. My youngest (now eleven) has very little contact with her dad so I know my appropriate physical affection is important to her. I think I can navigate this with her as I did with my own daughter, who is now older and married. Physical affection is prickly as they mature, whether they are your biological child or not. I sense that I'm much more careful about displays of affection when I'm alone with one of the girls and a little more prone to show appropriate affection when Mom is in the room. Having my wife there seems to lower the awkward-ness and perhaps the danger. It just seems safer."

Next, to make sure that your well-intended actions or affections are not misinterpreted, apply this principle: Let your stepchildren set the pace for affection in the relationship. When you aren't sure if a child is ready for physical affection (and emotional, for that matter), take your cues from them. If a ten-year-old jumps in your lap during movie night, she is telling you what she is comfortable with. If, on the other hand, you go to kiss a seventeen-year-old on the cheek before bedtime and she shudders, take note. For whatever reason, she is not ready for that level of affection. Next time, try a side hug (not face-to-face), and see if that is received more comfortably.

I first wrote about this in my book *The Smart Stepfamily.* Jerry wrote to let me know it really helped in his situation. "Your advice about letting the child set the pace has been a tremendous help. I have two stepdaughters; their dad passed away about eight years ago. At this point one is a senior in college and the other is a senior in high school. Our relationship has progressed to hugs and a periodic kiss on the cheek. There are also times when the senior in high school will snuggle up to me on the couch. Letting them take the lead has helped this not to be awkward for either of us."

Jerry's joy in being able to share his affections with his stepdaughters brings to light the point of this chapter. You have so much to offer your stepdaughter in the way of nurturance, affection, affirmation of her spirit as a woman of God . . . the list goes on and on. That's why Satan would much rather sabotage these positives by confusing the physical aspects of healthy expressions of love. He wants you to withdraw so he can keep you at an ineffective distance. Don't do it.

STEPSIBLING ROMANCE AND SEXUALITY

Online Chat Question: "We aren't related. He is my stepdad's son and a little older than me, but I think that he is really REALLY hot. I want to know if it would technically be okay for me to sleep with him."

Reply: "He's not your brother at all. Go for it."

I don't know about you, but I find the above forum dialogue very disturbing. The Internet is, of course, full of misguided advice; that much doesn't surprise me. But what did surprise me was how quickly I found myself reading this chat discussion (one search and one click) and how frequently I found a similar tone to other online conversations. Historically speaking, stepsibling romantic connections have been just as common as the stepfather-stepdaughter abuse cases we hear so much about. But with this kind of readily available encouragement, I fear the number of occurrences will rise significantly in the years ahead.

Craig talked to me at a conference. "I can't believe my daughter and her stepbrother, Josh, are telling us they have romantic feelings for one another. Even though Josh doesn't live with us, they have grown up knowing one another; my daughter was two and Josh was three when Carri and I married. How can this be? I guess they have already kissed at this point. What do we do?"

Brad and Gwen had been seriously dating for about a year when they discovered that her son and his daughter had a crush on each other. A friend told Gwen that the talk at school was that if Brad and Gwen got married, their children would be living in the same house—and they already liked each other.

Robert wrote to our ministry with a very heavy heart. "We are going through a storm and need some guidance. Marsha and I have been married for four years with four children and feel we have a healthy family situation. That's why we cannot understand why this has happened. My son Ian (age seventeen) and Marsha's daughter Monica (age fifteen) had sex last Sunday night. They have been like brother and sister throughout our marriage and now they have lost their virginity to each other. I'm just glad guilt took over and they confessed within a day. We have asked for help from our youth pastor and have talked with the kids about their decision, but we know this has changed our family forever. How could this have happened? We were proactive in teaching our children about healthy sexuality and God's values. What do we do now?"

In a moment I want to deal with Robert's questions of how this could happen and what they should do about it, but first let me calm your fears. Stories like these do not mean that boundaries will be crossed within your home. I said earlier that the incidence of stepsibling romantic attraction is just as common as stepfather-stepdaughter abuse, but that doesn't mean either is common. It's important to keep some perspective. Statistically, these circumstances are rare. There really isn't solid research to pinpoint the rate of occurrence among all families, but I do believe it to be uncommon. However, this type of behavior is more likely to occur in stepfamilies than in biological families. (I'll explain why in the next section.) Here's the point: Don't stick your head in the sand. Be aware of what could happen and take preventive measures to keep boundaries from being crossed.

"But why?" I can hear someone object. "Why try to prevent this? It's not incest." The first half of this chapter dealt with the matter of stepfather-stepchild sexual behavior, and that meets the definition of child abuse (if not incest). Laws around the globe in most societies declare it illegal. In addition, Scripture is very clear that it should not occur. The Holiness Code of Leviticus 18 makes it clear that people should "not have sexual relations with both a woman and her daughter. . . . That is wickedness" (v. 17). So, too, sexual relations between half-siblings is sin: "Do not have sexual relations with your sister, either your father's daughter or your mother's daughter, whether she was born in the same home or elsewhere" (Leviticus 18:9). But stepsibling sexuality is another matter. It is not mentioned in most laws that define incest, and not specifically detailed in Scripture as wrong behavior (or in most other major religions, for that matter). Perhaps it should fall under the general admonition to not have sex with "any close relative" (Leviticus 18:6). But then again, it isn't specifically mentioned in the rest of that chapter, which seems to define what "close" means (and goes so far as to mention a mother's sibling's spouse).

There are still some matters that are not clearly black or white. We seek God's wisdom about them, try to use common sense, and do the best we can. There may not be legal or biblical laws to apply here, but common sense would dictate that this is something we should discourage and guard against.*

Have you ever heard the maxim about dating, "Once you've had sex, you can't go back to being just friends"? It conveys that once sex enters a relationship, it changes the nature of the relationship.

---

*I am only referring to mutually romantic stepsibling attractions here. If one child is considerably older than the other, or if there is manipulation or aggressive behavior by one child, it should be considered abusive. Report this to proper authorities and get help.

Stepsibling sexuality would most certainly do that, so might a one-time kiss. The relationship would be forever changed, and so might the family. Even if the stepsiblings broke up, family members would be reinterpreting every message or interaction and tiptoeing around that part of the family narrative forever. And if one parent felt their son or daughter was victimized or manipulated in the process, it might divide the marriage and family with thick walls of resentment and protectiveness.

Needless to say, this is not something you want to see happen in your home. But what if it already has? Before dealing with that, let me outline why intra-stepfamily sexuality happens in the first place.

Understanding the Vulnerability

Being a stepfamily does not automatically manufacture sexual temptations, violations of trust, or benign stepsibling attractions. So why is this an issue in stepfamilies at a level unseen by biological families?

In *The Smart Stepfamily* I devoted an entire section to the dynamics surrounding sexuality in stepfamilies. Let me summarize those key points here.

- **No Natural Taboo.** Biological family members have a natural taboo against sexuality. It seems that shared DNA is a powerful deterrent to sexual attraction; this is one reason why incest is so rare. Ask someone if they ever have sexual fantasies about their parent or brother or sister and they'll say, "No way, that's gross!" That is the taboo barrier in action. Stepsiblings don't have shared DNA and therefore no natural taboo. This doesn't necessarily open the door to sexuality, but it does unlock it.

- **The Command for Closeness.** When two families come together there is an assumption that people will bond. The expectation and hope that stepsiblings will move emotionally toward one another with nonsexual displays of affection, warmth, and hugs can inadvertently encourage sexual curiosities that, if unmanaged, can draw kids across undefined sexual and psychological boundaries. The difficult teenage years of developing sexual awareness lend themselves to natural curiosities that may be applied to stepsiblings.

- **A Sexually Charged Environment.** This occurs in stepfamilies for a number of reasons. First, during your courtship, your children observe your developing couple romance. Some children even coach their parents on how to act and talk, or even what perfume to wear on a date. This awakens their interest in romance and sexuality. In addition, your children are often witness to the increasing physical affection between you and your soon-to-be wife. By the way, they may not like your shared affection and may speak out against it; nevertheless, it is simultaneously adding to the sexual messages of their world.

  But the influence doesn't stop there. After your wedding, their lives are freckled with even more romantic gestures from their parent and now stepparent. When added to their own developing sexuality and dating interests, children are surrounded by romance and messages acknowledging sexuality.

Parental Affection

Parent-stepparent affection adds to a sexually charged environment. Early in a stepfamily kids are often annoyed by it, but they aren't afraid of becoming the target of unwanted affections from a stepparent, for example. Interestingly, compared to boys, teenage girls in new stepfamilies are most upset by parental affection. To reduce this strain on the children, avoid sexually suggestive conversations and exaggerated affections toward your wife; choose wisely the movies you watch as a family so as not to create awkward situations.

- **Developing Teenage Sexuality.** Adolescence is a tumultuous and confusing time for most of us. Our bodies and hormones change, which increases insecurities; we experience romantic feelings and relationships that are foreign to us; and we are trying to understand our sexuality and how to manage it from a spiritual perspective. Teens are sorting through all this and more while being inundated with confusing and misguided sexual messages through a variety of media outlets. If left on their own to cope, teens sometimes make choices in their confusion that are not healthy. Which is, of course, why they need us as parents to discuss these issues with them and offer wise perspective and counsel.

• **Poor Boundaries, High Stress.** All of the above factors are unlikely, in and of themselves, to manufacture intra-stepfamily sexuality. In addition, stepfamily structure all by itself is not sufficient to produce increased risk of sexual behavior. But when these factors intersect with parents who are weak in setting psychological boundaries for themselves and others, new relationships with unclear boundaries and values, and a home with high levels of stress between family members (especially between the married couple), there is a negative synergy that exaggerates sexual vulnerabilities.[3] That's why your home needs boundaries that bring honor to God and to all the family members.

Healthy Boundaries, Healthy Attitudes

When you work with your wife to proactively communicate boundaries that encourage mutual respect, the risk of inappropriate sexuality diminishes significantly. Here are some practical suggestions. Talk with your wife about who is best positioned to speak with boys or girls, biological kids or stepkids in your home.

• Communicate God's value of all people and our need to respect physical personal boundaries. This healthy sexual attitude will apply not only to non-family members but stepfamily members, as well.

• Have house rules that honor personal privacy. Commonsense dress codes go a long way toward communicating your beliefs, values, and how to respect one another. Early-adolescent and adolescent girls, for example, should not walk around the house dressed for bed in their underwear and a long T-shirt, and teen boys should not walk to the bathroom in their boxers. It may be comfortable, but it invites the imagination.

• When setting dress codes, use the opportunity to teach about healthy sexuality and what arouses the opposite sex. For example, girls often underestimate how powerful visual stimulation is for boys (men). Tight or revealing clothes invite unwanted attention, even from stepbrothers.

- Insist that family members knock before entering bedrooms, and decide how persons will share the bathroom.

- Reviewing these boundaries is particularly important when part-time stepsiblings come for visitation or when a child moves to your home full time. Children and teens who have known each other for years, but never lived together full time, need clear rules of conduct.

- Tune in to discomfort. If you perceive a child withdrawing or showing signs of stress, calmly approach the child to investigate the situation. Ask specifically if they are feeling uncomfortable with romantic or physical boundaries.

- Talk about sexual attractions in a matter-of-fact manner. Acknowledging, for example, that sexual attractions between stepsiblings can occur normalizes them for the child. This is not to give permission to them, but to teach a proper perspective. The alternative is to say nothing and leave the child to determine the meaning of a passing thought or attraction, or to give negative messages that needlessly shame children. ("How could you think something like that about her? That's disgusting.") Being open about this, on the other hand, reduces the power of the thoughts or attractions.

Instead, you might say something like the following. First shared in *The Smart Stepfamily*, this script has helped thousands of parents have frank conversations with their son or daughter. This example is written for boys. "You know, as we talk about sharing the bathroom with your stepsisters, it occurs to me that some kids in a stepfamily like ours sometimes have passing sexual thoughts about their stepsiblings. If that ever happens to you, it doesn't mean you are bad or a disappointment to God. There will be lots of times in life that you have sexual thoughts or feelings toward other people, but it would be inappropriate for you to act on them or keep thinking about the person in that way. So if it happens, ask God to help you to stop thinking about your stepsister in that way. And make sure you don't dishonor her by acting on the attraction or thoughts. If the thoughts keep happening and you get concerned about it, feel free to talk to me. I won't be angry. We'll find a way to handle it. Any questions?"

But What Do We Do Now?

"That's all well and great, Ron, but lines have already been crossed by kids in our home. What do we do now?"*

Matthew called asking for guidance. He had just been blindsided by his fourteen-year-old stepson, Blake, who had confessed to having romantic attractions to his stepsister, Matthew's seventeen-year-old daughter, Brianna. Thankfully, Matthew didn't panic or react angrily to Blake, who had taken a real risk in sharing his feelings. No physical boundaries had been crossed, but Brianna, who was aware of Blake's feelings, was very uncomfortable about it and didn't want to find herself in the house alone with Blake. I talked with Matthew and coached him to calmly have a series of conversations with Blake. First he normalized that unwanted attractions sometimes occur in stepfamilies, but he emphasized that they should not be acted upon. Next they talked about managing sexual temptations in general and how not to entertain inappropriate thoughts. And finally, Matthew used the situation to ignite ongoing conversations with his stepson about biblical manhood.[4] The situation made family life very thorny for a season, but over time, trust was restored because Matthew and his wife did not look the other way.

Appropriate parental response will be different given the specifics of every situation (e.g., ages of children involved, whether it is a one-sided attraction or if sex acts have occurred, etc.). Remember the story I told earlier about Robert's son Ian (seventeen) and

---

*These suggestions do not apply to situations of abuse (one child considerably older than the other or rape). Seek outside help and counsel for such circumstances.

Marsha's daughter Monica (fifteen) losing their virginity to each other? Because sexual lines had already been crossed (making the same behavior easier to replicate), Robert and Marsha would have to respond decisively and with clear boundaries. I shared with them the following guidelines for family restoration and prayed with them. More than a year later I checked in with them to find out what the outcome was; I'll share their response with you later.

Each Parent Should Take Primary Responsibility for Their Child. You will need to have many discussions with your children about what happened, how it happened, what they are feeling toward one another, and how you will manage the relationship in the future. Spend lots of time talking as a couple to make sure you have the same expectations for the children from this point forward, then communicate them to your child. You might share these expectations together, but it's usually best in high-stress situations to let each biological parent talk individually to their child. This will not be a one-time conversation. Sexuality has many emotional, psychological, spiritual, and familial consequences. You will be processing these consequences and life lessons for a long time.

What About Everyone Else? You will have to decide as a couple how to manage the rest of your family. Are there other siblings who are aware of the situation? How will you include them in future boundaries and rules of conduct? I believe the entire family should know at some point (decide carefully how many details to share), but at what point should they know? Discuss this carefully and don't move ahead until you agree as a couple what the course of action should be. Also consider whether you will tell extended family members. Why or why not? There is no universal answer to these questions; each will have to be based on your circumstances.

Decide Together What Consequences to Impose. Helping children learn from their decisions sometimes involves punishment. Decide together how you will respond to what has happened and follow through. Be sure, however, to balance your discipline with reinforcing statements of love and assurance. Overreacting in anger and shaming a child without messages of acceptance can drive them further into sin.

Make Sure Physical Boundaries Are Clear. If you haven't been proactive in establishing a dress code or rules to manage physical boundaries (e.g., "knock before entering someone's bedroom"), you must do so immediately. The emotional chaos and anxiety that will result from sexual lines being crossed will necessitate structure and clear boundaries for everyone. You may have to get even more specific with rules. For example, "John and Julie cannot be alone in the house together for a while; we'll have to coordinate schedules to make sure this is honored." Having said this, try to avoid going into complete control mode as parents, but provide insulation where you can.

Try to remove temptations. Remember, sex doesn't have a reverse gear, only forward. In other words, once kids have had sex, doing so again becomes a lot easier even if it was "accidental" in the first place.

The most awkward boundary to discuss is future physical affections. As family members, stepsiblings may share hugs, hold hands during family prayers, and say "I love you." Though they were once celebrated in the home, these common family affections will now be considered suspect. Children cannot go back to a time of innocence. They need to be able to express appropriate affection, yet doing so may be confusing. Again, biological parents will need to plan for many "check-in" conversations with their children to see how they are feeling about such matters over time. In addition, you'll have to ask yourself how you will know when your fears are exaggerating the circumstances. All of these issues will need to be discussed as a couple and sorted out over time.

And what about affections between other family members? In one family when two teens engaged in a solitary romantic/sexual touch, it dramatically affected the couple's marriage. Not wanting to encourage repeated behavior by the children, the wife became fearful of showing her husband affection both publically and privately. A temporary response such as this is understandable, but over time this has the potential for real harm in a marriage. Guard yourselves from becoming victims of your anxiety.

Have "What If?" Conversations. These are aimed at changing behavior in the future and helping children have a plan. The possible conversations are numerous. Getting the conversation started is your job; once started, the child will lead you where you need to go.

- "What if you two find yourselves at home alone? How will you handle it?"
- "What if you feel attracted to him/her again? What will you do?"
- "What if someone brings this up and you feel embarrassed? How will you act?"
- "What if you feel pressured by your stepbrother/sister?"

These types of questions help a child take responsibility and develop an action plan for the future. Some parents are tempted to tell a child what to do and how they will feel. In highly emotionally charged situations like this, doing so—especially with teenagers—usually backfires. Help them think it through with you and come up with their own strategies. Your job is to coach their thinking process toward maturity.

Engage in "What Have You Learned About Yourself?" Conversations. These conversations are aimed at helping the child grow through this experience. You wish it didn't happen, but it did. Help them learn something about themselves.

- "What made you vulnerable to this situation?"
- "What were you thinking when you began undressing?"

- "In what ways did you rationalize or justify your behavior?"
- "You know that being stepsiblings makes this very complicated for our family. How did you dismiss that when you pursued the relationship?"
- "How will you manage your vulnerabilities in the future?"

Pursue Healing. Inappropriate sexual behavior will bring many negative consequences. Commit yourself to the God who offers healing, and seek it for your home. It's probably wise to seek out a trusted counselor, pastor, or mentor to offer guidance as you pursue forgiveness and restored trust. The process may not be easy, but by all means don't give up.

I promised you a report on Robert and Marsha's situation. A year after their storm hit, they reflected on what was helpful to their healing.

We have indeed weathered the storm. We held fast and have been restored as a family. We were so taken aback and felt so broken when it happened, but, wow, God really showed up. It is nice to look back and see how God comforted and directed us through the trial.

At first Marsha and I thought our family would never be the same. But we never spoke of defeat, only victory. We instantly told our children that they were forgiven and that we were extending to them the same grace we had been given. (God helped us say that because inside I wanted to knock some heads!)

We used your suggestions and developed some boundaries. At first when my daughter and stepson were in our home they had to retreat to their bedrooms when we went to ours. There was to be no interaction between them while we were in bed. Thankfully this was pretty easy because they saw their mistake and were uncomfortable being around one another. We also insisted that they never be home alone.

We asked the questions you suggested: What were you thinking? Did you think how these actions would affect those in our family? What have you learned through this experience? Both of them were open and very sorry. The conversations gave everyone insight into how this happened and how to prevent it from happening again. I asked them to write an apology letter to us and to each other. They included thoughts on how to repair their relationship into a brother-sister type relationship. They came up with some good boundaries on their own and a plan for how they could repair their broken trust with one another. Over time they have become relaxed and able to have fun watching movies or playing games as a family.

Looking back, I think the most important thing we did was show them grace and forgiveness right from the very beginning. We let them know we were hurt, but through it all we still loved them. Climbing this mountain of recovery has been difficult, but it has made us stronger as a family.

IS THERE SOMETHING WRONG WITH US?

I really hate bringing up matters of sexuality when it comes to stepfamilies. Not that it makes me uncomfortable; I speak regularly on marital sexuality when conducting conferences around the country and have not hesitated to talk one-on-one with my three children about sexuality. What I dislike is how this subject makes people shrink in shame.

In previous years when I would speak to parent audiences about these sensitive issues, people would squirm in their seats and stare at the floor the entire time. And I understand why. Yes, the general topic of sexuality makes people uncomfortable, but specific topics like stepfather sexual abuse and stepsibling romantic attractions are particularly distressing—in part, I think, because it implies that stepfamilies are somehow dirty or immoral. "If we weren't a stepfamily this wouldn't have happened in our home," said one parent referring to the newly discovered stepsibling attractions going on in his home. "Is there something wrong with us that this could have happened?" Do you hear his shame?

Every family has vulnerabilities. The stepfamily has more sexual vulnerabilities than does the biological family, but that doesn't invalidate the legitimacy of your home. The Evil One wants to stigmatize and make your family feel illegitimate so that he can erode your sense of moral rightness and togetherness. Sexual vulnerabilities lend themselves to these insecurities and the judgment that "something is wrong with us." But don't throw out the proverbial baby with the bathwater.

I believe that as husband and father/stepfather, you have the obligation to protect your home. We protect those who live in our homes from worldly influences, from unhealthy practices, and from misguided decisions. We do so, for example, by discerning which media sources (books, videos, music, Internet) we will allow to influence our children or by encouraging our children to select different friends if the ones they have are leading them away from Christ. We also protect our homes by guarding our marriages and following God's guidance on how we spend our money. And we protect our homes when we uphold sexual fidelity and battle the very notion that the family itself is wrong simply because it has unique sexual vulnerabilities. Don't let the presence of temptation confuse you into thinking you lack God's blessing. Without question, such temptations should be managed and prayed through, but don't let the deceiver use them as ammunition to destroy your family solidarity. Stay the course; keep climbing.

HEROES BY CHOICE

For Group Discussion

1. Talking about these sensitive subjects can be difficult. Renew your commitment to one another not to repeat information shared during your meeting with people outside the group. Be safe for one another.

2. Can you relate to any of the stepfather-stepdaughter situations presented in the chapter?

3. Even if you have never experienced this temptation, what can you learn from Sean's strategies for sexual purity? Apply them to maintaining purity with any woman.

   - He admitted his vulnerability.
   - He didn't minimize the potential destructive impact of improper actions.
   - He made a "covenant with his eyes" not to look.
   - He moved his eyes away from temptation.

4. How can you refrain from withdrawing in fear too far from a stepdaughter, and thereby communicating rejection to her?

5. Stepfather-stepdaughter romantic or sexual activity is clearly wrong, sinful, and inappropriate. What is your opinion of stepsibling romance?

6. Review the section Understanding the Vulnerability, beginning on page 178. Which of those dynamics are true in your home?

7. Discuss the Healthy Boundaries, Healthy Attitudes section. How can you apply these?

8. If stepsibling romance/sexuality has occurred in your family—and you feel safe enough to disclose it—discuss as a group the But What Do We Do Now? section. Remember to maintain confidences for one another. Pray about the situation together.

9. Sexual vulnerabilities make some people feel shameful about their stepfamily. Remind each other that the Lord has always used and blessed individuals and families that were less than ideal, even some that were sexually sinful (e.g., King David and his family). How can you remind yourself to stand firm in God's grace?

Chapter 11

Keeping Special Days Special: Holidays, Vacations, and Your Stepfamily

As with so many things, if Mom and you are in
agreement, then you can just go for it.
Even with an intact family there can be a lot of grumbling
about vacation plans. Usually everyone enjoys the
experience once it's underway.

BOB

If you ask me, Bob just nailed the essentials of climbing this portion
of Stepdad Mountain. First, find unity—and thereby, strength—
with your wife. Second, realize that all families have grumbling and
complaining when it comes to vacations and other special days. And
third, keep some perspective. When it's all said and done, usually
family members enjoy the experience once it begins. Having said
that, there are, of course, a few unique struggles faced by stepfamilies

when planning special days, holidays, and family vacations; these factors deserve a little attention and planning:

- Feeling like an outsider. Getting a birthday card is nice, but when it comes with a dutiful attitude or when compared to what the biological dad or siblings get, it can feel like a slap in the face.

- Blender expectations. If you or your wife feels increased pressure to make the holiday ooze with family togetherness and affection, you may try throwing everyone into the blender. The increase in pressure may blow up in everyone's face, especially if strained steprelationships already exist.

- Ex-spouses. Everyone wants their time and plans to take precedence over the other household, so otherwise cordial negotiations with ex-spouses may escalate into war before holidays.

- Increased kid stress. All of the above ripple into the hearts of kids, who feel and reflect the tension in the household. Plus, increased loyalty battles that come from being caught in the middle may result in increased depressive symptoms or acting out, causing even more parental concerns.

WHY THE STRESS?

There are certain times in stepfamily life that naturally increase tension and bring to the surface issues that otherwise can be avoided; special family days are a good example. Why? Because such occasions carry high hopes and high expectations of family togetherness. Celebrating someone's birthday or gathering for Thanksgiving dinner is supposed to be a memory-making activity, one that honors the past and celebrates the present. This can be a recipe for disaster for some stepfamilies (but not all by any means), especially those who find themselves still in the early years of developing relationships and a family identity. Increased pressure during the special day to "cook the family" means the blender gets taken out of the cupboard, even if someone has to get creamed in the process.

> **For Mom**
>
> How does your desire for family harmony and peace increase your "blending" efforts during the holidays?

Andy, stepdad to Meredith and father to Jason, found himself getting creamed. His wife, Carly, and her ex-husband communicated pretty well about the holidays and vacations. When his stepdaughter was young they lived close enough to one another that Meredith would split holidays like Christmas or Thanksgiving with her father. But when Andy, his wife, and their son, Jason, moved farther away, Meredith would spend Christmas week and about eight weeks in the summer with her dad. Andy and Meredith had a strained relationship, so the new arrangement seemed like a win-win to him; Meredith got a lot of time with her dad, and Andy got to relax and enjoy his wife and son. "I really loved the time that Meredith was with her dad—in fact, I relished it. It gave me time to connect with my wife and my son without jealousy, competition, or any emotional games."

That all changed before Meredith's junior year in high school. Carly wanted Meredith to get a summer job and live with them full time. Andy shared, "My wife's decision to have her daughter with us for the WHOLE summer was devastating to me. The summer was my time of healing and recuperation following ten months of dealing with all the ugliness of my stepdaughter. In my humble view, she could easily have gotten a summer job with her dad, but Carly wanted her with us. It was a very brutal two years until she went away to college."

Plus, Andy got the news that Meredith was no longer going to be spending Christmas with her father. "What really hurt is that these decisions were made without my input."

This story highlights the powerlessness that stepdads sometimes feel. Even though Andy had a strong say in what happened with his son, he didn't have much influence at all in the arrangements made by his wife for his stepdaughter. This is frustrating without a doubt. I wish I could present an easy black-and-white solution that would fix all such circumstances—for example, "Moms should never make unilateral decisions" or "Stepdads should never resent a child who has little choice over their summer visitation schedule"—but such solutions rarely hold up under the scrutiny of life. Rather, the principle for parents to apply is to communicate a lot about the circumstances with which you are presented, and find a way to bring grace to the situation for each other and for the children.

But another fundamental dynamic revealed in this story pertains to the issue of emotional closeness and distance between insiders and outsiders in stepfamilies. A poorly developed stepdad-stepdaughter emotional attachment and a strained relationship led Andy to prefer that Meredith not be with them during holidays and the summer months. He felt relieved when she left and described his wife's decision to have her with them all summer as "devastating." I am willing to bet that her mother didn't use such words in her description of the situation. As insiders with their children, mothers have a much greater tolerance for their children; as an outsider, it is understandable that a stepdad won't. Andy's insider relationship with his biological son, Jason, made the contrast even more profound. Exclusively being with his wife and son at Christmas was to be free of jealousy, competition, and ugliness. And then there was Father's Day.

"For about ten years Father's Day was always a bad day for me when my stepdaughter was home. She would get me a card but it was more of a token to please her mother, not a genuine gift for me. When Meredith was younger she seemed very jealous and mean-spirited on Father's Day. She would barely talk to me. Honestly, I didn't want her around on Father's Day. Why should she ruin my day? I didn't care if she celebrated it or not, I just wanted to be with my son and wife for the day. But my wife suffered from a 'Brady Bunch' belief that we were all going to be together and happy for

How to Cook a Stepfamily

- Blender mentality: when adults who innocently hope to facilitate relationship between stepfamily members place high expectation on children to feel love or affection for others. This pressure often results in more resistance to bonding, not less.
- Crockpot mentality: when adults acknowledge that different ingredients will combine at a unique pace and that it takes years for stepfamilies to develop a sense of family identity. Adults are intentional to encourage relationship building but relaxed about the timing. They also are not afraid to compartmentalize the family into sub-units (e.g., mom and her children) for certain occasions.

For more read *The Smart Stepfamily.*

Father's Day, even though her daughter was hostile at times. Of course, I was angry at my stepdaughter for this, but I was also angry at my wife for not protecting that day for me."

Did you hear it? Carly had a strong blender mentality that would kick in around the special days. She believed that forcing togetherness would push Andy and Meredith through jealousy toward love. It didn't. In fact, it made things worse. Adopting a Crockpot mentality in regard to special days, summer visitation, and holidays might have saved everyone a lot of grief. I can't predict what specific decisions Carly and Andy would have made, but applying a Crockpot perspective might have opened options to them such as alternating annual Christmas schedules with her ex and letting Meredith spend every Father's Day with her dad. The point is that special family days bring to the surface the tension around togetherness and family identity. Family members—biological parents in particular—become extra sensitive to the movement of family members toward or away from one another. They may fear movement away (e.g., letting Carly spend Father's Day with her dad) as a sign of family failure or disconnection. But it isn't necessarily. It simply acknowledges that some family members are closer to some than others, and it gives people freedom to honor their traditions.

TRADITION, TRADITION, TRADITION!

Traditions are important because they tell us who we are (i.e., provide a sense of identity), give us solid anchors on which we can depend, and give security to the future. When traditions clash between stepfamily insiders and outsiders, it shakes these foundations and generates insecurity. A statement like, "My family always serves Thanksgiving dinner late in the evening. I'm sorry if your kids have to leave before then—that's just too bad," is testimony to someone's loyalty to their extended family and shows insecurity in giving up an anchor. "That's just too bad" also reveals the insider/outsider nature of the stepfamily's relationships.

Adult Stepfamilies

Older and adult stepchildren have a strong vested interest in preserving family traditions. It doesn't feel like "going home" if they can't count on certain traditions taking place. Make changes very slowly!

Let's face it, we all like to keep some things constant in life. Even naturally flexible people tend to prefer predictability in family traditions. And when added to the numerous changes and adjustments required of stepfamily members, changing just one more thing—a tradition, no less— might result in an emotionally charged reaction from someone.

Try to have compassion for the person (maybe it's you!) who has this reaction. Remind yourself that the tradition being challenged is important, and so is the meaning tied to it. Try to help family members retain important traditions. And when something must change for the greater good of the family, be patient and compassionate with the loss.

Here is, by the way, the good news about traditions. For the same reasons adjusting or losing traditions is stressful, building new ones is a tremendous opportunity for you to further your sense of family identity. Each repeated tradition, such as birthday celebrations, anniversaries, and holidays, helps to solidify your family story. The first time you go on a family vacation it is a new adventure (it may not even turn out well). But the fourth time you go on an annual vacation it is "something we do every year." Feel the difference? Yes, you may have to endure a few rocky starts, but don't give up on the process. Eventually the wet concrete will solidify and give you something firm to stand on. So live and learn from your mistakes. Keep refining your negotiation skills. Apply compassion when needed. And keep going!

PRACTICAL STRATEGIES FOR KEEPING SPECIAL DAYS SPECIAL

Now that you understand what's at stake, here are a few suggestions to help you and your family move in the right direction.

Celebrate the Reason for the Season

Whatever the holiday, special day, or event, try to stay focused on the celebration at hand. Negotiating details and wrestling with hurt feelings can easily distract you from the purpose for the day. Despite all the drama, bring your enthusiasm and joy to the celebration of the birthday, anniversary, or holiday—even if the arrangements are not as you would like. Bring a positive attitude, and a celebration just might break out.

Plan, Negotiate, and Plan Some More

Jack shared his stepdad insight to keeping special days special. "First, make sure you and your wife are fully united on the vision and plan. Then, build buy-in with the kids early," he said. "We start talking about plans and potential plans early in the year so that the kids will get the vision of where and what we are considering." Proactive planning is critical, especially when there are multiple homes, multiple parents, and lots of extended family to engage.

Don't wait till the last minute. "If you do not get along with or communicate well with the exes, it is a hundred times harder," shared
Danny, stepdad of four, "and the kids will without fail get caught in
the middle." He went on to share that when you can't have cordial
negotiations with an ex-spouse, you might have to stick strictly to
the divorce decree. At least that provides an objective standard that
everyone should adhere to.

There are a couple things you can do to help kids accept and
contribute to the plans. First, give your verbal permission for them
to enjoy the time they spend with other family members during
the holidays. As we discussed in chapter 4, when you tell children
and stepchildren alike that they are not being disloyal to you when
they enjoy the people in their other home, it releases them from
guilt and paradoxically moves them closer to you. Ultimately this
creates a warmer climate when it comes time to implement your
plans for the holiday or special day.

Next, when teenagers are in the mix, be sure to give them a
chance to contribute to the plans. The older children are, the more
input and influence they need to have in family planning. To encourage buy-in, let them have a voice.

One aspect of negotiating with the other home is choosing your
battles carefully. Decide what your nonnegotiables are and then
look for ways to compromise on issues that aren't. For example,
you may have to open Christmas gifts a day or even a week before
Christmas in order to get the time you'd like with the kids. Opening
gifts together is a nonnegotiable; when you open them isn't.

Choosing your battles with an ex-spouse includes discerning
whether a battle is worthy of being fought or dropped. If your ex-
husband-in-law, for example, is normally pretty flexible about holiday schedules, but for some reason one year he is not, let it go. Likely
some other dynamic is at play in his life and his stubbornness is a
one-time behavior. If, however, he is adversarial and selfish when
it comes to the children most of the time, you may need to take on

a battle in order to establish a more reasonable arrangement. This may require the use of an attorney, the legal system, etc., and comes with great risk and cost, but in the end is probably worth it so you don't have to deal with the same issue next time.

Let me offer one final word about planning. In the early years of stepfamily life, the tentative nature of emotional attachments may mean it is wise to compartmentalize some holidays. You and your children, for example, may spend Thanksgiving with your family while your wife and her children spend it with hers. Of course, this doesn't feel good to those with a blender mentality, but it may be just what the doctor ordered. Attempting to blend every person and every tradition prematurely may create bad memories that have to be undone later. Spending a portion of the first few holidays apart may result in further family success later on.[1] Communicating this decision to extended family members may be awkward, so remember the old adage that "blood talks to blood." Your wife should talk to her extended family and you to yours; each of you should also be responsible to communicate this to your ex-spouses.

Avoid Comparisons

Getting caught up in comparing household traditions only exacerbates loyalties and resentment, as does comparing financial circumstances. Whining that the other home always goes on a holiday cruise while you can't afford to just makes kids feel guilty about enjoying the trip. In turn, they tend to resent you for making them hide their joy. Don't put kids in the middle of your financial differences. If necessary, feel free to set boundaries about how money is spent. For example, grandparents might need to be informed of a price limit for birthday gifts so that children with different grandparents are treated equitably. Don't let some children live high off the hog while someone else eats from the trough. And finally, if the children are the ones comparing (and they will), encourage them to celebrate with others what they have. Talk with them about guarding their hearts from envy and demonstrate how to do so for them.

Father's Day

I once asked a group of stepfathers this question: Father's Day is just around the corner—how are you feeling in anticipation? I'll never forget Bob's answer. "I'm not really looking forward to it. I don't like the pressure it puts on my stepkids. I and they know I'm not their dad, but if they don't do anything for me, how are they supposed to feel? They're stuck either way."

Many writers, including Emerson Eggerichs in his book *Love and Respect,* have articulated well a man's need for respect and appreciation. We guys thrive on it. Even if our wives are confronting something in our character they don't appreciate, if they speak respectfully, we're more apt to listen and take it in. Even sex falls in this category if you ask me. We make lots of jokes about the physical pleasures of sex, but what sex gives us is so much deeper than that. It communicates value, our wives' desire for us and admiration of us. Among other things, it strokes that deep psychological cord within us for appreciation and respect.

Father's Day is a day of appreciation. It encourages all of us to express the value we place in our father. That's what makes it so awkward for both stepdads and stepkids. The confusion of your role, children's loyalty conflicts, and the family's journey to build family identity collide on Father's Day. Just how are they to honor you? How do they say thank-you without hurting Dad's feelings? If they give you an inch, will Mom get all excited and expect them to treat you with appreciation all the time? (The fear of this happening is enough for some kids to hold back their gratitude.)

I appreciate Bob's comment above because his concern is more focused on the awkwardness of the day for the kids, not so much himself. I'm sure on some level he hoped for some recognition of all that he had done for his stepkids, but he focused instead on how stuck they might feel between him and their father. One possible course of action would be for him to simply be open with them. He might say something like, "Hey guys, I know Father's Day is coming up soon. If I were you, I'd be concerned about having to do something for me—and figuring out what is appropriate could be awkward—and yet giving your full honor to your dad. He certainly deserves it. You might even be worried a little if he will be hurt if you get me a card or something. Just know that I believe you should honor your dad. And whatever you do for me is cool with me."

This type of conversation helps take some air out of the balloon before it pops, but more important, it opens up the possibility of many more honest conversations about the kids being caught in the middle, divided loyalties, etc. When your family runs from these realities, everyone suffers. When you boldly engage them in these realities, you make it easier for the family to cope.

One final thought: It will get better. When asked that same question about anticipating Father's Day, one stepdad with six years under his belt said this: "In the past I had quite a lot of anxiety over not wanting to dishonor or take away from their relationship with their biological father. It has been an uncomfortable feeling, wanting affirmation for the role that I play but not wanting to force an emotional response out of the boys. Actually, I have not felt much stress about it this year. We are coming up on six years of marriage; I suspect that a familial bond has set in." Looks like he is nearing the top of Stepdad Mountain.

> ## How Churches Can Help
>
> When churches and social groups acknowledge step-fathers around Father's Day, it helps to affirm their role in modern families and challenges the stereotype of the abusive stepfather. It also encourages stepchildren to value you. I encourage pastors to use this simple script on Father's Day—pass it on.
>
> "This morning is Father's Day, a time to honor the gift of our dads. If you are a father, a stepfather, an adoptive father, a foster dad, or a man who cares for or mentors children not his own, would you please stand so we can honor you this morning."

Keep Something Old, Find Something New

Part of the balance of stepping into your wife and stepkids' traditions is letting them keep as much of their past as possible, while working with your wife to create something new that is unique to your family. Bringing some of your traditions to the table is helpful, but the goal is to insert something entirely new for everyone into the special day. Established traditions from both sides have a tendency to compete; new elements of the tradition are uniquely "us." For example, Scott encouraged his wife and kids to celebrate their birthdays just as they always did before he came along. And in addition, at a family meeting they all decided to post the day's events on Facebook (something Scott knew a lot about). This added some excitement to the day and let Scott be the focal point for the added tradition. Each birthday reinforced the new family tradition and the new family.

Water and Ducks

Finally, take some good advice from ducks. They know how to let water glide off their backs—and do so with grace. There will be lots of frustrations, points of contention, and feelings of isolation that come with holidays, special days, and vacations. Whenever possible, let it slide.

HEROES BY CHOICE

For Group Discussion

1. Can you relate to any of these experiences when it comes to the holidays or special days?

   - Feeling like an outsider
   - Blender expectations (increased pressure to come together)
   - Ex-spouses (otherwise cordial negotiations with ex-spouses escalate into battles during the holidays)
   - Increased kid stress

2. Review Andy and Meredith's story beginning on page 193. What aspects of their situation apply to you?

3. What traditions did you, your wife, and the kids have in common from the start? What traditions are you building together?

4. Review the list of Practical Strategies for Keeping Special Days Special. Which are strengths in your home and which need improvement?

   Celebrate the Reason for the Season
   Plan, Negotiate, and Plan Some More
   Avoid Comparisons
   Keep Something Old, Find Something New
   Water and Ducks

5. Is Father's Day something you look forward to? What anxiety or tension seems to rise when this day rolls around?

Chapter 12

Romancing Your Wife

I love it when my wife smiles an "I'm so glad I married
you" smile. I get such a rush!

JASON, STEPDAD TO FOUR

"We missed out on the 'honeymoon period,' including the bonding
that occurs before children," Josie shared. "I feel like I was robbed of
being romanced and 'wined and dined.' On our wedding day we left
the chapel for the reception and low and behold there were five of us
in the car; my husband and I in the front seat, and my daughter and
his two daughters in the back. Instant family. For some strange reason I didn't see that coming. Silly me, I thought we'd actually be able
to drive alone! The first few months of the marriage I had irregular
breathing and heart palpitations due to anxiety. I was overwhelmed
with the instant family and the lack of time together as husband
and wife. My husband was hurt because he thought I wasn't happy.
I did think through the new family dynamic, but I didn't anticipate
it would affect me to the degree that it did. It was a sea of emotions
that I didn't see coming."

Stepfamily stress can easily crush fairy-tale dreams of marriage and riding off into the sunset. Dana shares, "Every girl secretly dreams of a handsome prince who is consumed with undying love for her. I just knew mine would sweep me off my feet. He showed up all right. But he was carrying three children with an ex-wife following close behind. I'm sure he thinks my kids and ex are just as cumbersome." When couples feel overrun and discouraged, romance suffers.

> ### For Mom
>
> What romantic fantasies did you have before marriage that have been challenged by stepfamily living? Read this chapter and talk with your husband about how you might implement some of the tips for keeping romance alive in your marriage.

This is not to say that a stepfamily marriage will be void of romance and passion. As in all marriages, couples in stepfamilies must make an effort to keep the romance alive and growing beyond the initial chemistry that first brought them together. Sustaining love requires commitment and dedication. Intoxicating stares and passionate sex don't remain unless the couple works at it. I've long thought that the reason fairy tales end with the wedding is because the author didn't know how to write the rest of the love story. Accomplishing "happily ever after" is more difficult than a storybook implies. But it can be done.[1]

TIME FOR ROMANCE

> During courtship, couples naturally find time to dance. After the wedding, couples can easily fall off the dance floor.

Have you ever noticed that a dating couple cherishes the time they have together? They anxiously await precious moments when they can enjoy each other's company. Couples instinctively know that building a connection with someone requires talking, listening, exploring, and enjoying each other. Dating is often purposeful, goal oriented, and fun. In contrast, marriage is often invaded by the demands of children and tasks. Add complacency to the mix and the relationship can become dull and aimless, resulting in partners who take each other for granted.

One mark of a healthy relationship is the ability to overcome marital lethargy by energizing the relationship with focused amounts of time. Feeding the relationship with enjoyable activities and nurturing time together provides fertile ground for the marriage to thrive. A weekly or bimonthly date night can be a relaxing way to spend time together. A periodic extended date such as a day trip to a neighboring town or a Saturday afternoon of leisure activity can revitalize your marriage. Twice a year get away from home and stay overnight in a hotel. This requires planning and a little money, but it provides a healthy atmosphere unlike anything you can create at home. And don't forget your wedding anniversary. Try to do something memorable every year to properly celebrate the special day.

Erin shared how she and her husband maintain connection. "We make a point to hold hands, hug, kiss, and just be close. For us, just knowing the other is near helps to relieve stress. We carve out time to spend together, making each other a priority. Our friendship helps a lot; it's important to like each other, as well as love each other."

ACTIVATE YOUR FUN FACTOR

In a survey of over 50,000 stepfamily couples, Dr. David Olson and I uncovered a very important treasure for stepcouples that we dubbed the Fun Factor.[2] This study examined fifteen aspects of marriage (e.g., communication, sexuality, spirituality, relations with family and friends, etc.). We discovered that of all the factors, nearly 20 percent of what accounted for a highly intimate stepcouple relationship was shared leisure activity. In other words, a regular dose of fun is a huge contributing factor to marital health, stability, and satisfaction.

In one portion of the survey, couples who were thriving advised other couples to "take time to be together away from the kids" and "re-energize your marriage with enjoyable experiences." Our study discovered that the happiest couples respected each other's unique interests and hobbies, but also prioritized shared activities over individual ones. In contrast, couples with the weakest relationships were three times more likely to be dissatisfied with the amount of fun in their marriage.

> ### Smart Dating
>
> Make note of what you enjoy doing together. Drifting away from fun activities is somewhat natural after marriage. Discuss a few ways you plan to implement enjoyable activities once you are wed.

Further, when comparing the strengths of first marriages to those in stepcouple marriages, our research discovered that shared leisure time and fun is more significant for stepcouple success than for first-marriage success. The survey did not reveal why this is true, but one theory I have is that because stepfamily life is inherently more stressful than biological family living, stepcouples need something to ease the tension. The antidote to the stress factor just might be the fun factor. Be intentional, then, about engaging in activities that bring pleasure and enjoyment to your marriage.

Shared Fun

One key aspect of the Fun Factor is that leisure time be spent together. In other words, leisure time spent apart doesn't count. Craig is an avid golfer. He plays a round of golf every chance possible. He also watches golf on TV and purchases a new set of clubs every two years. His wife, Michelle, enjoys running and wood carving. Each spouse respects the other's preference and "covers the bases" at home so the other can enjoy their hobby. However, Craig and Michelle rarely do anything together. Their separate activities provide personal enjoyment and aid physical health, but a lack of shared leisure activity will negatively impact their marriage.

Finding Time

At the beginning of their relationship, Craig (the golfer) and Michelle (the runner) did share fun times together such as dinner and a movie. But the pressures and the frenzy of family, work, church, kids' sporting events, and other responsibilities have squeezed out this crucial element. If they desire a healthy marriage, they would be wise to restore and recover what has been lost.

> ### Adult Stepchildren
>
> Finding time to be together is much easier when you have adult stepchildren. However, convenience can become complacency. Empty nest couples sometimes report that frequent time together is easily taken for granted. On occasion, go the extra mile when planning dates or activities to add a little spice to your time together.

What activities did you and your wife enjoy together before you got married? It's possible that there were fewer kids around or that her visitation schedule conveniently carved out time for you to be together. Regardless of the reason, it's important to discuss with her ways you can proactively restore those opportunities. This might require adding a few dollars into the budget for activities or baby-sitting. If you are serious about creating a solid marriage, it's not a luxury but a necessity. And leisure time doesn't need to be expensive; it can be as simple as bowling or a trip to a coffee shop, zoo, or art gallery. Even a nearby park can provide a much needed sanctuary. The point is to spend time together, not necessarily to spend money.

KEEPING ROMANCE ALIVE

Adding fun and romance to your marriage is essentially about injecting the relationship with energy. This can be accomplished in a multitude of ways. Just think of things that make either of you smile.

> ### P.D.A. (Public Displays of Affection)
>
> Even biological children sometimes get "grossed out" when parents hug or kiss. Your stepchildren may experience additional negative feelings when they witness affection between you and their mother. Be sensitive to their feelings, but small doses of affection are okay.

Sexual and Non-Sexual Touch

Every marriage needs sexual passion, but playful affection without a sexual agenda is one way to add vigor to your relationship. Now hold on, guys, I know sexual connection is generally a high priority for us men, and you would like nothing better than for me to tell you how to bring more sex to your marriage. Ironically, that's just what I'm doing by telling you to initiate non-sexual touch more often. Let me explain.

> "Our intimacy is deeper and our sex life more fulfilling because we are real, genuine, and honest with each other. We pray together, and that in itself is a great act of foreplay!"

The message communicated by non-sexual touch (e.g., warm hugs, holding hands while riding in the car, spooning in bed) is one of affirmation and value. You are telling your wife how much she means to you. That connects to her heart and strengthens her sense of security. The message of sexual touch when in balance with non-sexual touch is one of passion and pleasure. But if a woman receives only sexual touch from her husband, the message changes to a negative one. She associates affection with your sexual needs and your selfishness; she feels used in the process. Nothing will reduce a woman's sexual desire more than feeling that she only matters to the extent that she can fulfill your sexual needs.

That's why a healthy balance of sexual and non-sexual touch is so important. Each conveys its own positive message and makes way for the other. When you regularly engage her in non-sexual touch (instead of her having to force it upon you), it opens the door for other times of sexual passion.

For years I have been encouraging couples to engage in a thirty-second kiss challenge. The challenge is simple: Spend the next two weeks offering your spouse a thirty-second kiss every day. Why thirty seconds? Because most couples slip into a complacent pattern of engaging in either hello/good-bye kisses (lasting a millisecond), or kisses while engaged in sexual intimacy. They no longer kiss as a way to connect and stir passion (which sometimes includes sexual arousal but not always). A thirty-second kiss takes a little effort, but it can energize the connection and warmth for one another. By the way, don't tell your wife about this idea before you start. Just do it and see how she responds.

Bedroom Dancing

Now that I've said that, a healthy sexual relationship is also an important aspect of marriage. Of course, finding time and energy is sometimes an issue. For some couples, stepfamily living presents them with convenient opportunities to engage in sex; for others it presents constant barriers.

Opportunities:
- Occasionally not having any kids in the house gives couples time and opportunity to relax and focus on their lovemaking.

- Many stepcouples are past childbearing and don't have to deal with infants or small children who require a high degree of physical and nighttime care.

Barriers:
- Parenting stress adds to couple stress, which makes sexual connection more difficult.

- Having extra children on the weekends adds activity and increases fatigue, which can reduce sexual energy.

If alone time comes naturally for your stepfamily, take advantage of it and send up a thank-you to God. If it doesn't occur naturally, become proactive in carving out time for intimacy. Sex is not everything in a marriage, but it is vitally important in order to maintain closeness.

Cohabitation

At the root of many cohabiting relationships is fear. Couples choose the halfway house of cohabitation in order to have the benefits of living together without the emotional and financial risks of marriage. The irony, of course, is that cohabitation itself has been shown to bring about the very things that couples fear: relationship distress and breakup.[3] I encourage couples to seek God's best for their relationship by not cohabiting. This will honor God's will for their life and help them keep an objective perspective about their relationship. Remember, love is blind and sex is a blindfold.

Finally, strive to enhance your sexual connection. Learn all you can about healthy sexuality, and recognize the differences between sex in a first marriage and remarriage. Most people think they know a lot about sex because they read an article in *Cosmo* or have seen a number of steamy movies. But in my experience, most couples are very unaware of sexual functioning, eroticism, and pleasuring techniques. To get informed, it is very important that you consult the right resource (there is a lot of junk literature regarding sexuality). I suggest you reference my book coauthored with David H. Olson titled *The Remarriage Checkup* and Doug Rosenau's book *A Celebration of Sex* for more on this topic.

Be Captivated With Her

In Proverbs 5, Solomon cautions his son to avoid the enticements of the adulteress, that is, any woman who would steal his interests or affections. "Her steps lead straight to the grave," he says (Proverbs 5:5). In contrast, Solomon concludes the chapter by encouraging his son to focus his affections on his wife.

> May your fountain be blessed,
>   and may you rejoice in the wife of your youth.
> A loving doe, a graceful deer—
>   may her breasts satisfy you always,
>   may you ever be intoxicated with her love. (Proverbs 5:18–19)

There is nothing a woman thirsts for more than feeling that her husband is captivated with her. When her entrance into the room causes you to freeze with a monumental smile as you gaze at her beauty, she knows you have eyes only for her. When you take the time to really listen to what she is saying—and reflect what you believe it to mean to her—she trusts that you cherish her worth in your life. And when you study her habits, preferences, or interests so you can join her or cater to them, she glows with the security of knowing you are captivated by her.

Then the fountain of romance will flow freely between you.

Celebrate Your Wife

- Be accessible to her. Tell her where you are and how to reach you.
- Tell co-workers that you can be interrupted when she calls.
- Speak well of her in public and hold her close when an attractive woman enters the room.
- Repeat your wedding vows often.
- Compliment her regularly.
- Send flowers, write love notes/emails, and take care of small tasks so she doesn't have to.
- Attend a marriage conference together. Show her that you are willing to learn and deepen your intimacy.
- Say "I love you" before she does.
- Pray with her and for her while she listens.[4]

Meet Her Romantic Needs

In their book *Starting Your Marriage Right,* Dennis and Barbara Rainey share what they consider to be the top romantic needs of a woman. In a way, their list summarizes what has been presented so far, but it also adds a significant depth to what I've shared. The Raineys successfully cut through all the surface-level fluff of romance to what really matters. I'd like to share their thoughts with you here.[5]

A Woman Needs to Be Spiritually Ministered to by Her Man. In my mind, spiritually ministering to your wife includes two key aspects: serving love and protective leadership. The apostle John tells us that after loving his disciples for many years, Jesus showed them the full extent of his love: He removed his outer clothes, bowed a knee, and washed their dirty, stinky, nasty feet. This is serving love. The humility that is demonstrated by Jesus not only served the immediate need of the disciples (clean feet), but more importantly it communicated his love and commitment to them. This compelled them to love and appreciate him in return. When you seek to serve your wife with everything you are—even if it means taking on great sacrifice—you solidify in her heart your dedication to her. And you invite her to reflect a similar dedication toward you.

Spiritually ministering to your wife also includes protective leadership. Looking out for the family requires us to be decisive at times; not for the selfish purpose of overpowering others to get our way, but in a protective way to guard against unhealthy influences that would harm our marriage or family. When your wife watches you stand up for what is right, just, and honorable, she will view you as a "soul protector" for both her and her children. To do so, of course, means knowing yourself what God's will is for your home. This means engaging your wife and yourself in Bible study and Christian activities that deepen your walk with the Lord.

A husband who is dedicated to these tasks is likely to have a wife who feels safe in his care, trusting of his heart, and willing to give up anything to keep him close to her side.

A Woman Needs a Man Who Will Share Intimate Conversation. Over the years of conducting marital and sex therapy with couples, I have heard this complaint from husbands again and again: "My wife has sex with me, but rarely does she make love to me." What these men are experiencing is a wife who engages in sex at the physical level but not at the emotional and spiritual level. One guy said, "Having sex with a sterile, disengaged warm body gets old very fast. I need to connect with her, not just her body."

Verbal intercourse to a woman is the equivalent of sexual intercourse to a man. It is the place of connection, affirmation of the relationship, and where she feels valued by you. If I asked your wife whether you actively engage her during conversations or if she is "having intercourse with a dry, disengaged lover," what would she say? Learn to prioritize intimate conversations. Men are really good at sharing facts, but strive to share your feelings, as well. Open the door to your thought life and heart. Giving her access to this will help her to feel connected and intimate with you.

A Woman Needs to Receive a Tender Touch and Hear Gentle Words. Earlier I talked about how non-sexual touch affirms a woman's sense of worth and value. Likewise, tender words and gentle responses (even when irritated with her) are a verbal "tender touch." Praise your wife for her actions and her character. Compliment her femininity, charm, appearance, faithfulness to God, hard work, and dedication to her (and your) children.

A Woman Needs to Be Pursued and Set Apart by Her Man. Dennis and Barbara say, "A wife wants a husband who will swoop her off her feet, carry her away to the castle, and say, 'Let's spend time together.' Focused attention is like precious gold in a relationship."[6] For years Successful Stepfamilies has been run out of our home. A small ministry with very little revenue, we just couldn't afford office space large enough for both Nan and me and our resource inventory. Mostly we used our garage and basement to get the ministry started. What this meant practically was that I was never too far from work and often found myself checking messages or attending to details during evening hours. This made Nan feel unimportant because everything else seemed to get my attention, but not her or the kids. She was right.

I addressed this by setting firm boundaries with my time (no going in the home office after 6 p.m.) and refocusing my attention on her and our kids. Giving up my need to stay on top of work tasks was, in effect, a pursuit of my wife. So, too, is it when I turn down speaking invitations that would generate revenue for our family but take away from our family time and life balance.

You and I make hundreds of decisions every week that prioritize our wives or something else. Of course, not everything can be centered on her. But clearly you want her to know that you are continually pursuing her heart. I frequently joke that we men are hunters. We see something we want so we hunt it down and conquer it. Perhaps you, like me, did that when trying to win the heart of the woman who is now (or will become) your wife. Dating and courtship are the "hunt" for one woman's affections. But once you caught your limit, have you stopped hunting her? She hopes not.

WE'VE LOST THAT LOVIN' FEELING

What do you do if you've lost the romance? Entire books have been written on that subject, and there isn't space to include a comprehensive discussion here. But perhaps I can offer a summary of what must happen to restore the romance.

In Revelation 2, John is told to confront the church at Ephesus about forsaking their first love. A church that had once lived out their deep abiding love for Jesus, they had become distant and cold toward him. John writes, "Consider how far you have fallen! Repent and do the things you did at first" (Revelation 2:5). John's prescription for restoring spiritual love is also a good map for restoring romantic love in a marriage.

First, remember. If you and your wife have lost your romantic connection, remember that there was a time when you had a handle on this. What brought you to that point? How is it that you fell in love to begin with? Rediscover the reasons you pursued her and what attracted you to one another and see if you can't start again.

John's admonition to remember how far you have fallen could also be interpreted as urging them to realize how distant they have become. Sometimes romance suffers because we men are not in tune with the emotional distance between us and our wives. We can be so consumed with our careers and aspirations that we drift many miles from our wives without even realizing it. That's one reason I am such a believer in the online Couple Checkup inventory that is designed to affirm couples' strengths and point out weaknesses (*www.CoupleCheckup.com*). If there is distance in your marriage, it will show you just how far apart you are and what needs to change. My book *The Remarriage Checkup,* coauthored with David H. Olson, includes a free individual Couple Checkup voucher so that you and your wife can save on the cost of the inventory. The book then guides you through a process of building on your relationship strengths while overcoming your deficits.

John's second step is to repent. Literally meaning to feel remorse or regret over one's actions to the point of making a 180-degree turn in the other direction, repentance is the point of change. To say you regret the lost romance in your marriage is nothing without a change of heart and action. This leads to John's third step in the prescription: Do the things you did at first.

In what ways did you serve your wife at one time that you no longer do? What actions and attitude used to characterize you that don't any longer? Begin again to do these things—even if it doesn't make sense to do so. For example, if you and your wife have drifted so far that your thoughtfulness is received by her with suspicion, keep being thoughtful. You will be tempted to give up in defeat. "What's the use?" you might say to yourself, "she doesn't give me any credit for it anyway." This thinking most definitely brings defeat. Don't give up and don't quit doing what you did at first. Now is a good time to be stubborn—lovingly stubborn.

As Christians we believe that Christ will always take us back, no matter how far we've moved away from him. Grace takes us back. If you and your wife are struggling, I wish I could guarantee you the same result. I can't. But do everything within your power to bring healing to your marriage. Seek wise counsel; surround yourself with friends and family who believe in your future together; and humble yourself before the Lord. Restoration is worth it.

HEROES BY CHOICE

For Group Discussion

1. How has the dynamic of "instant family" challenged your couple time and romance?

2. Consider this quote: "Dating is often purposeful, goal oriented, and fun. In contrast, marriage is often invaded by the demands of children and tasks." How can you remain intentional about nurturing your couple relationship?

3 Share your current Fun Factor couple activities.

4. What insights did you obtain from the section about a woman's need for balance in sexual and non-sexual touch?

5. What challenges do you have to finding time alone?

6. If you are cohabiting, assuming you see the wisdom of reestablishing sexual purity and living in separate residences, how can you go about making that a reality?

7. Review and discuss the top romantic needs of women as stated by Dennis and Barbara Rainey.

   - A woman needs to be spiritually ministered to by her man (this includes serving love and protective leadership).
   - A woman needs a man who will share intimate conversation (verbal intercourse to a woman is the equivalent of sexual intercourse to a man. It is the place of connection, affirmation of the relationship, and where she feels valued by you).
   - A woman needs to receive a tender touch and hear gentle words (this affirms a woman's sense of worth and value).
   - A woman needs to be pursued and set apart by her man (focused attention is like precious gold in a relationship).

8. If your marriage is drifting, what can you do to remember, repent, and restore the things you once did in order to recapture your first love?

Chapter 13

Adult Stepchildren

An adult son said to his father after a Christmas
gathering, "You spent more time getting to know
her children and grandchildren than with our side of
the family. Are you ready to love her children
just as much as you love us?"

Climbing Stepdad Mountain is a lot easier when you aren't travel-
ing with minor-aged children, but don't be too quick to assume it's
easy. There are a number of unique dynamics to adult stepfamilies
that can add challenges.

This chapter targets adult stepfamilies that initially formed after
the children were adults (over the age of eighteen). It is certainly true
that stepfamilies formed with minor-aged children will have unique
challenges after the children become adults; however, I am limiting
the discussion here to the unique transitional issues associated with
adult stepfamilies.

Warning and Word of Caution: If you saw this chapter title
in the table of contents and started reading here, I strongly advise
that you begin with chapter 1. Most of the key principles addressed

throughout this book apply to adult stepfamilies, too. The specific complaints from adult stepchildren are somewhat different from those of younger children (e.g., inheritance issues); however, the essential feelings, fears, and concerns are very similar.

The principle of patience, for example, is important for adult stepfamilies. It's possible you may need even more patience than younger stepfamilies since "cooking time" is dependent upon how much time you spend with the stepchildren. Some adult stepfamilies are spread out across great distances, which makes it even more difficult to build relationships. In addition, the matters of loss and loyalty (chapters 3 and 4) are just as salient for adult stepchildren as they are for younger children. Other principles, such as those addressing parenting, may not apply to your situation. But in general I encourage you to consider the entire book valuable information for your family.

If your wife was widowed, you may be tempted to dismiss principles that seem to apply to divorced families. Again, most principles have application to you and your adult stepfamily. Those of you who skipped several chapters in this book and zeroed in on this subject will likely walk away feeling that pieces or solutions are missing. That's because many of the dynamics of adult stepfamilies are addressed in other chapters. Be sure to go back and read those.

BECOMING AN ADULT STEPCHILD

Barrett met Gabrielle through an online dating service. Both divorced empty-nesters with active careers, Barrett had three adult children and Gabrielle two. Gabrielle had a complicated divorce and an ex-husband who often put guilt trips on their children. Accordingly, Gabrielle's relationship with her kids was strained. When she started dating Barrett, her children pulled back even further. Then, just two weeks before the wedding, her oldest son, age twenty-nine, announced that he wasn't coming. Gabrielle was crushed and Barrett felt horrible for her.

Common Reactions and Feelings

Why would a child make such a decision? He must have been put up to it by the ex-husband, right? Perhaps, but maybe not. Here are a few of the common reasons why adult stepchildren struggle with a parent's later-in-life remarriage. Please note that these reactions may apply to your children as well as your stepchildren.

Loss and the Fear of More Loss. After losing one parent to death, or the family to divorce, children at any age fear losing what remains. Some adult stepchildren fear abandonment or isolation from their parent. When the children must share their mom with you, it means a loss of her time and energy. This is especially true if the stepdad has children or grandchildren who also occupy the mom's time. This fear is often expressed as anger or resistance in developing a relationship with you.

Smart Dating

Time is your friend. A rapid dating-to-engagement period increases the likelihood of resistance and negative feelings from adult children. You may be ready, but remember, a wedding will send emotional ripples throughout the generations. Go slow.

Adult children appreciate being informed about a regular dating partner. Don't keep them in the dark as your relationship progresses. This breeds suspicion and a lack of confidence in your decision to marry.

Also, because your time horizon is different from that of adult children, you may think a long engagement is a waste of time. However, try to balance your desire to move ahead with the children's need to adjust to a changing family identity.

If you and/or your wife are the recipient of anger, resistance, or guilt trips from adult children, remember that these responses are probably rooted in fear. Acknowledging those fears and *ministering* to them can help to ease the tension.

Betrayal. For some children a remarriage feels like a betrayal of the other biological parent. This is true in divorce as well as death, in particular if the children see their dad struggling with health issues or loneliness. They may have the viewpoint, "Sure, Mom, your life with a new husband has turned out great, while Dad has lost everything." Children are especially likely to have this attitude if their dad is suffering because of choices made by your wife. If your stepchildren feel that they or their dad have been abandoned, encourage your wife to hear their pain, apologize for the role she may have played in the divorce, and seek reconciliation. While you cannot fix these problems, you can encourage her to restore a relationship with her children.

When Dad Is Deceased

If the biological dad is deceased, maintaining a strong family identity by preserving the family name, keepsakes, assets, and mementos is a great way to strengthen the adult stepfamily. Most likely the kids have experienced a disruption of life's continuity; therefore, any choice by the mom or stepdad that jeopardizes the original family structure or values may be viewed as betrayal.

Jealousy and Rejection. Jealousy is the fear of being replaced. Close cousins to jealousy are resentment and competition. Some adult children feel replaced by a stepdad. That causes them to compete with you. And let's be honest; you *are* taking their mother's attention, time, and energy, and they want it back. Your initial response to this may be, "My stepdaughter is an adult; she needs to move on and be happy for us." However, criticizing a child's feelings won't build a bridge. Instead, put yourself in the child's shoes and empathize with their pain.

A Smart Stepdad would say something like, "Susan, I know you and your mom are close; it must be hard to watch me step into the picture. I know it can never be exactly the same as before we got married, but I want you to know that I want the two of you to continue to do special things together. As a matter of fact, I noticed in the paper that a local art gallery is having a Monet display next month. I know you love art and so does your mom. Why don't the two of you go?"

As a stepdad this communicates four things:

1. I recognize your pain.
2. I admit that things are different, but I hope to work toward a solution that benefits everyone.
3. I am actively seeking ways that you and your mom can stay connected.
4. I am not insecure or competing for your mom's time and affection.

Concern Over Family Finances. Adult stepchildren are often concerned about family finances, in particular when their biological father has died. And well they should be; concerns over family inheritance and assets are legitimate. A Smart Stepdad knows how to resist the temptation to minimize these concerns or label them as greed. Adult children have the right to know how your marriage is going to impact a college fund, inheritance, and significant family keepsakes. Be proactive in addressing these matters.

Be sure to revisit your financial arrangements in order to address both your long-term provision for each other and the adult children's financial concerns. In his book *Money and Marriage God's Way,* Howard Dayton of Compass Finances God's Way suggests that couples proactively reexamine financial plans before marriage. It is advisable for you to consult an attorney and financial planner who are well-versed in remarriage and stepfamily finances. For example, you may need to change the beneficiaries of your life insurance

> **For Mom**
>
> The fears associated with betrayal and family loss run deep. If you haven't recognized these issues in your children until now, make a plan to respond to them. One idea is to spend time with your biological family by yourself whenever possible. Spending time alone with a child or grandchildren might be all it will take to help everyone see that you are not disappearing from their lives. Reassure your husband that you need this separate time with your kids to help your marriage find support for the future. Ask him to graciously give you these occasions.

policies or change the ownership of car titles or deeds to a home or other property. New wills should also be drafted to reflect your changing circumstances.

As a general rule I do not recommend prenuptial agreements as they may plant seeds of distrust in a couple's relationship. However, a good alternative is what my friend and financial advisor Greg Pettys calls a Shared Covenant.[1] This written agreement is designed for couples whose marriage will form a stepfamily, and it clarifies emotionally charged issues for the couple and their children. You can provide details, for example, of how you and the children will be provided for should their mother die and you remarry. Proactively addressing these matters and communicating a provision to the children can help to ease fears often associated with money and inheritance. When possible, allow stepchildren to contribute to wording of legal documents so they feel some influence over the process. Fears increase when decisions are made in secret.

It's All in a Name

Initiate a conversation to discuss what terms or names you will use to refer to one another. Find something mutually comfortable.

- Don't insist they use terms of endearment for you (e.g., "Dad"), but if both of you are comfortable with it, that's fine.

- Discuss how you will introduce each other in public (e.g., "This is my wife's son, Mark" or "This is my stepfather-in-law.").

- Discuss what names you will encourage grandchildren to use. Young stepgrandchildren may use uncomplicated terms of endearment since they bond more quickly. But if "Grandpa" feels awkward to the adult stepchild (grandchild's parent), find a variation that suits everyone (e.g., "Papa Joe").

The above emotions and reactions will determine the temperature of your family Crockpot. Understanding and acknowledging the circumstances is the first step to learning how to respond appropriately. Here are a few suggestions.

SMART STEPS FOR STEPDADS OF ADULT STEPCHILDREN

1. **Discuss with your wife any negative emotional reactions exhibited by her children.** When a child expresses betrayal, anger, or alarm over your relationship, encourage your wife to speak to the child alone and say something like, "Your anger yesterday tells me how much you love me and about the concern you have for our family. I appreciate that very much. I, too, love you very much. I can only imagine how my new marriage is causing you confusion. I expect that you are worried how this will affect our relationship; could we get together again to discuss that? I'd like to hear more of what you're feeling."

2. **Listen to negative feelings and reactions with humility and openness.** The worst mistake a mom or a stepdad can make is to imply that the child has no right to feel a certain way. An adult stepchild should not be allowed to insult, berate, or abuse you. Those responses are unacceptable and your wife needs to step in and confront the rudeness. But if the child is expressing negative emotions, the best response is to listen non-defensively. Express humble compassion and validate the difficulty of this transition.

For Mom: Preparing for a Wedding

Engage in "feed-forward" conversations to help children anticipate changes for your family after a wedding. These conversations also let you know their feelings. For example:

- Before an engagement ask your kids: "It's one thing for me to be dating; how do you think you'd feel if I became engaged?" "What would that mean to our family?"
- Before a wedding: "This is going to change a lot in our family's life. I expect that you are concerned that I'll have less time for you and the grandkids. We also need to talk about your inheritance. What are you thinking about these matters?" "What do you hope will never change in our relationship or family?"

Keep this type of conversation active over time. Adjusting to significant life change requires an ongoing dialogue between family members.

3. **Communicate the No-Threat Message (from chapter 8) to your adult stepchildren as well as your ex-husband-in-law.** Say, "You only have one father and I am not him. Please know that I understand I could never replace your dad, nor will I try. I also realize that you may feel confused about my place in your life, and I can appreciate that. I hope that we can be friends; I'm willing to do all I can to make that happen."

4. **Extend the hand of friendship whenever possible.** Remember, you are a parent in name only. Take interest in their lives; learn about their professions, children, and hobbies; engage in recreational activities; and try to be supportive of their personal goals and family.[2]

5. **Connect through the grandchildren.** Engaging with your stepgrandchildren, who often bond quickly with stepgrandparents, can stir warm feelings for the entire family.

6. **Prepare for holidays, celebrations, and family traditions.** Dialogue about transitions: "I realize Thanksgiving may feel different this year since my family is joining us. I apologize if this takes time away from your family. Would you like to plan some special time with your mom?"

7. **Work toward clearing the air.** If there have been hurtful words or hurt feelings on either side, attempt to build a bridge of forgiveness and humility.

8. **Be patient with adult stepsibling relationships.** Your children and her children may find middle ground upon which to be friendly with one another, but it may take a while. Give them opportunities to connect, but don't attempt to force a bond.[3]

9. **Offer compliments and affirmation to your adult stepchildren.** Words of encouragement and kindness can go a long way toward building relationships.

10. **Don't feel guilty if adult children treat you like "the father they never had."** Trust that they are capable of knowing what they need from you.

When Dad Is Deceased

Celebrate his memory. The paradox is that while you keep his memory alive, it lowers the family's resistance to you and increases respect for you.

* From time to time, ask about their father and listen to the stories.
* Offer the family time to grieve together (e.g., an annual visit to the grave; ongoing conversations about life before and after his death).
* Anticipate occasions that resurrect grief (e.g., Father's Day, his birthday) and find ways of openly acknowledging their hurt.

For further reading on this topic, I suggest *When Your Parent Remarries Late in Life: Making Peace With Your Adult Stepfamily* by Terri P. Smith with James M. Harper. While this book is written for the adult stepchild, it gives later-life couples perspective on what their children are experiencing and how to manage the marital transition. You can also share it with your adult stepchildren. This may stimulate much-needed conversation about the family transition.

HEROES BY CHOICE

For Group Discussion

1. In what ways did you assume (and hope) that being an adult stepfamily would be easier than having young children?

2. How is physical distance from your stepchildren or life circumstances a help or hindrance to your growing relationships?

3. Review the common emotions and reactions of adult stepchildren. Which do your stepchildren seem to be experiencing?

   Loss and fear of more loss
   Betrayal
   Jealousy and rejection
   Concern over family finances

4. Have you negotiated names or terms for how you will refer to one another in public and private? If not, how might you orchestrate this conversation?

5. Review the Smart Steps for Stepdads of Adult Stepchildren beginning on page 225. Discuss and apply those that are appropriate to your situation.

6. What other insights occurred to you while reading the chapter?

Chapter 14

Should We Have an "Ours" Baby?

My wife says it's normal for a woman to want to have
a baby with her husband. I'm not so sure I want more
children; she already has three and I have one.
That's enough for me.

BRIAN

Whether you've already had an ours baby or are considering it, you
may be wondering how adding a baby to a stepfamily impacts the family dynamic. The results of social research to date on this subject are
mixed; the answer is that we really don't know. In deciding whether to
climb this face of Stepdad Mountain, I suggest you carefully consider
the terrain as you pray for wisdom, and then make your decision.

CONSIDER THE TERRAIN

Here is some of what we do know about how the birth of an
ours baby impacts a stepfamily.

An Ours Baby and Your Stepfamily

You may have heard the theory that an ours baby creates a *concrete baby effect* that helps "cement" stepfamily relationships.[1] Sounds promising, doesn't it? The hope is that having a child gives everyone someone with whom they can equally relate. As one child said after his new half-brother was born, "At last, someone who is related to everyone." The only problem with the theory is that there is little research to support the idea.[2] Stepfamilies experience a wide variety of emotional and relational changes after an ours baby is born. Some are encouraging and some aren't.

The ours child has a greater chance of bringing a positive impact to the home when these factors are present before he or she is born:

- Relationships within the stepfamily home are generally stable and positive before the pregnancy.
- Children already have a positive relationship with their biological parent and stepparent.[3]
- Stepchildren live with the stepparent (and biological parent) full time (or the majority of the time).
- Children are young in age.[4]

When these dynamics are in place, half-siblings may consider the mutual child a full sibling, which can bring a great sense of joy to everyone. By contrast, adult half-siblings have widely varying relationships with an ours baby. Some are close and have frequent contact, while others are distant and neutral about the new child. Infrequent contact with the stepfamily, a lack of involvement, and the differences in age-related interests are common reasons for the emotional disconnection between a stepchild and the ours baby.[5]

If the relationships within the stepfamily home are generally divided between insiders (biologically related persons) and outsiders (steprelationships), a mutual child can bring further division. Biological children who already feel slighted may feel jealous of the time and attention a new child receives, thereby causing resentment toward a half-sibling.

Another factor to consider is the pressure that can be experienced by the mutual child. Being related to everyone puts this child in the center of the family's experience. This *hub* position, as it has been referred to by researchers, cuts both ways.[6] On the one hand, it is a privileged position that gains more attention than the other children (especially part-time children). This affords the child more influence and control in the home. On the other hand, this child may feel a constant pressure to create bonds between family members and ensure that everyone gets along.

> ## Smart Dating
>
> Having a child before a wedding is unwise for many reasons. First, sexual impurity dishonors God and loudly communicates wrong moral behavior to other children. Second, having a child out of wedlock facilitates an artificial commitment that often fails later. Third, sex before marriage can blind couples to weaknesses in their relationship. It fools them into believing they have a stronger relationship than they actually do. Honoring God's boundary that sex be reserved for marriage guards you from these dangers.

If you decide to have a mutual child, it's wise to refrain from communicating high expectations. This includes telling your biological children, the stepchildren, and the mutual child that he or she will "bring everyone together." If that happens naturally, then rejoice. If it doesn't happen, you don't want any of the children to feel they have failed the family.

An Ours Baby and Your Marriage

Did you know that when first-marriage couples have a baby it reduces their risk of divorce? A child strengthens the couple's commitment to one another. As one woman said, "I don't consider leaving my marriage because there's more at stake now." But there's a downside to having a child as well. Couples in first marriages experience a sharp decline in marital satisfaction during the child-rearing years. It seems the business of raising a child can take away some of the joys of marriage. Guess what? These two dynamics are also true for stepcouples who have an ours baby.[7]

The issue of whether to have more children should be discussed before you get married. Dating couples should not take for granted that their partner will have the same opinion as they do. If one of you wants another child and the other doesn't, will you continue dating? Will you get married? If both of you do want another child, how will you handle your differing emotional responses? If you don't have biological children, for example, you will have "first-time joy" when your child sits up, crawls, walks, talks, etc., but your wife may not (a common change in parents who have been through all the firsts with older children). How will you celebrate what you have in common instead of worrying about what you don't?

An Ours Baby and Parenting

There's nothing like the unconditional, unreserved love of a child. The first time your son or daughter calls you Daddy, your heart just melts.

Having your own child can be extremely fulfilling (this seems especially true for stepdads who do not already have a biological or adopted child). In chapter 4, I provided an explanation of parent-child attachments. This mutually beneficial relationship offers an automatic love, grace, respect, and approval between parent and child. Specifically, it is an attachment where you are an *insider*—always. That experience may be vastly different from your stepdad experience.

Not all stepdads will experience a stark contrast in parental fulfillment if they have their own child. But when an ours baby arrives, many stepdads do discover a vast difference in affection between the stepchildren and a biological child. This presents a trap to avoid. The ease of being Dad versus the challenge of being Stepdad can trigger a temptation to emotionally withdraw or create distance from the stepchildren.[8] This reaction communicates a message of rejection to the stepchildren, plus it can hurt your wife, and it lays the groundwork for resentment between half-siblings. Resist the temptation to pull away from stepchildren when a biological child is born. It's not abnormal to love your own child more than you do the stepchildren, but each child has the right to be treated equitably without favoritism.

By the way, there is another side to this dynamic. Some stepdads discover that having a child strengthens their affections and compassion for their stepchildren. After their own child is born, stepparents who had strained, distant relationships with stepchildren sometimes feel more secure and have more tolerance for stepchildren.[9] Another benefit to the family is when a stepdad recognizes that all children—even his own—act poorly at times. This can eliminate a judgmental attitude toward his wife and her kids. There's nothing like a good dose of reality to soften a stepdad's heart.

PREPARING FOR AN OURS BABY

If you are planning to have an ours baby, here are some suggestions to consider.

1. Expect ripples throughout your multiple-home stepfamily system. For example, a biological father who has been uninvolved in his children's lives, or disinterested in your family, may suddenly reemerge after you have a baby. Expecting change will help you cope when surprises arise.

2. Have lengthy conversations with all the children and extended family about how life will change after the baby is born. For example, anticipate how your family schedule will change (practical life change) when the baby is born,

plus how stepkids may feel envious that the new half-sibling doesn't spend time in another home (emotional change).

3. Try to keep half-siblings' lifestyle, visitation schedule, and parental contact relatively unchanged after the baby arrives.

4. Trust your intuition. If you anticipate harsh or negative reactions about a new baby from stepchildren (or your biological children), plan carefully how to prepare them. Don't just hope for the best.

5. Celebrate. When the children are excited about the new arrival, buy them "I'm the big brother" (or sister) shirts and encourage a family party.

6. To encourage the bonding between half-siblings, it's best to orchestrate frequent contact between the children.

When Dad Is Deceased

Contact the deceased father's extended family (his parents and siblings), and give them permission to be involved in the life of your child. Their involvement, for example, as "grandparents" in birthdays, holidays, child care, etc., bridges the insider/outsider gap in your home and blesses all the children with lots of love. Possessiveness divides, permission connects.

7. Raise all of the children with similar values. When half-siblings perceive inequalities in rules, expectations, the availability of money, or affection, they can become jealous and angry.

8. Refrain from being defensive or easily offended when stepchildren voice frustration or concern over how the new baby has affected them. If the relationship with your stepkids is strained, you will be tempted to assume every comment has to do with being a stepfamily. Note that older full-siblings in biological families commonly voice such concerns, as well. Sibling rivalry is normal. Not every expression is stepfamily rejection.

Marriage Adjustment

1. Expect that the addition of a child will result in less time for each other. While it may take a few months before you find

time alone, be intentional to carve out time for romance and friendship again soon.

2. If this is your first child, remember that your wife has been here before. Don't hold this against her, as it's normal for her to feel less excited about the "firsts." You may respond the same way with your own second child!

Parenting Adjustment

Every season of parenting requires couples to discuss their expectations and how they will share parenting responsibilities. It's possible that if your children and stepchildren are older, you may not have discussed how you will raise and care for an infant. Proactively talk through these matters as husband and wife.

For Mom

If you have another child, remember to equally invest yourself in all of your children. Staying connected with older kids may mean leaving your husband to care for the baby for a few hours while getting some one-on-one time with the others.

SO, WHAT SHOULD YOU DO?

It's obvious that I can't tell you whether you should or should not have an ours baby. It's tremendously complicated and there isn't a solid way to predict the outcome or the impact on everyone involved. However, one thing is vitally important: Examine your motives and your expectations, and be certain that having a child is not part of an unrealistic fantasy or an effort to control and/or create family harmony. It is unfair to burden an infant with that role.

Spend a season of time praying with your wife. Make this important decision based on love, the desire to raise a child, and the Lord's leading.

HEROES BY CHOICE

For Group Discussion

1. List your stepchildren and key extended family members (e.g., your mother, your wife's family, etc.). What are (were) your assumptions about how each of them will (would) respond to another child?

2. An ours baby has a better chance of being a positive influence on a stepfamily when these are true. Which are true for your family?

   • Relationships within the stepfamily home are generally stable and positive before the pregnancy.
   • Children already have a positive relationship with their biological parent and stepparent.
   • Stepchildren live with the stepparent (and biological parent) full time (or the majority of the time). Residential half-siblings tend to bond more deeply with the new sibling.
   • Children are young in age. Younger half-siblings adjust more easily than adolescent or adult half-siblings.

3. Have you ever known someone who was an ours baby and raised in the *hub* position? What was their experience?

4. What are the dynamics at play in your marriage around having a baby? What are the push/pulls (pushes toward or things that pull you away from it)?

5. Might you be susceptible to the temptation to emotionally pull away from your stepchildren once you have an ours baby? How can you guard your heart from doing so?

6. If you already have or anticipate having a child together, review the list of tips for Preparing for an Ours Baby beginning on page 233. Which can you apply to your situation?

Chapter 15

Heroes by Choice

*Being a stepfather to four stepsons is a lot of work,
but I only get one chance to build a man. I'd rather get
it right on the first pass and not leave a lot of remodeling
for someone else to deal with later. I want to
get it as right as I can.*

GERALD, STEPDAD TO FOUR BOYS

Stepparents often get a bad rap. The "wicked stepmother" and the "abusing stepfather" are stereotypes that just won't go away. But here's why you can let those harsh judgments roll off your back. They always come from people who are looking up from the bottom of the mountain. Once you, your family, and onlookers get to the top and look back down, the perspective is different. Very different.

Brad Paisley and Kelley Lovelace (a stepdad himself) wrote the song "He Didn't Have to Be" from the perspective of a child who had journeyed with his stepdad to the top of Stepdad Mountain. Looking back over the edge at the great distance they had traveled together and the challenges they had overcome, what we hear echoing over the mountaintops is the heart of a stepchild filled with gratitude. Before his stepdad came on the scene, the child proclaims, something was missing. But then they became a family. No stereotypes or harsh judgment, just appreciation for the blessing of a stepdad who didn't have to choose love but did. Someday, he concludes, "I hope I'm at least half the dad that he didn't have to be."[1]

Do you suppose Jesus had the same feeling about his stepdad?

I've long thought it a great injustice that Mary has received so much honor and attention throughout history for being the mother of the Savior while Joseph is hardly ever mentioned. We do know much more about her, so it is understandable. But what about the dad who didn't have to be? What if Joseph didn't?

But he did. He chose to love, care for, and claim the child he didn't father. And clearly he had a choice—he almost walked away. But at the Spirit's leading, he stayed. And the God of the Universe, who chose to give up heaven in all of its glory, power, and privilege in exchange for a cross, the Savior who chose to sacrifice himself for the sake of hope . . . was himself chosen by a humble stepdad.

Not many have sung the praises of Joseph through the ages, but I'm sure we can all agree, he is a hero.

May God bless you for climbing Stepdad Mountain. May God bless you for being a hero by choice.

HEROES BY CHOICE

For Group Discussion

1. Imagine the day when your stepchild(ren) sing similar words of appreciation over you. What will that day feel like?

2. What reminders do you need to help you press toward the top of Stepdad Mountain when the challenges are great and the rewards few?

3. Had you ever thought of Joseph as Jesus' stepfather? Discuss what that might have been like for him.

4. What inspiration can you draw from Joseph and his choice to love and be used by God?

5. No matter where you are now—at the bottom of Stepdad Mountain, in the middle, or nearing the top—look back over your climb. What challenges have been overcome already? What remain?

6. As a result of reading this book, what perspectives about your climb have changed for you? What wisdom would you pass along to another stepdad if given the opportunity?

NOTES

Section I: Getting It Right

1. P. C. Glick, "Remarried families, stepfamilies, and stepchildren: A brief demographic profile," *Family Relations*, 38 (1989): 24–27.

2. E. Thomson, J. Mosley, T. L. Hanson, and S. S. McLanahan, "Remarriage, cohabitation, and changes in mothering behavior," *Journal of Marriage and the Family*, 63 (2001): 370–380.

3. Susan D. Stewart, *Brave New Stepfamilies: Diverse Paths Toward Stepfamily Living* (Thousand Oaks, CA: Sage Publications, 2007), 61–62, 72–73.

Chapter 1: Conquering Stepdad Mountain

1. Stephen R. Covey, *The 7 Habits of Highly Effective People: Restoring the Character Ethic* (New York: Fireside, 1989), 98.

2. Personal communication. Jeff and Judi Parziale, *www.InStepMinistries .com*.

3. James H. Bray and John Kelly, *Stepfamilies: Love, Marriage, and Parenting in the First Decade* (New York: Broadway Books, 1998), 29.

4. Ron L. Deal and David H. Olson, *The Remarriage Checkup: Tools to Help Your Marriage Last a Lifetime* (Minneapolis, MN: Bethany House, 2010), 135.

5. Gil Stuart (father to four, stepdad to three) and his wife Brenda are trusted stepfamily educators. Together they have written *Restored*

and Remarried: Encouragement for Remarried Couples in a Stepfamily (Vancouver, WA: Seven Trees Media, 2009).

Chapter 2: Sex Stuff: Did You Marry a Wife (Sex Partner) or a Mother (Business Partner)?

1. Dr. David Olson and I shared a number of ways couples can enhance their sexual relationship in our book *The Remarriage Checkup: Tools to Help Your Marriage Last a Lifetime* (Minneapolis, MN: Bethany House, 2010), chapter 14.

2. Ibid., 217.

3. Barry and Emily McCarthy, *Couple Sexual Awareness* (Cambridge, MA: Da Capo Press, 2002).

4. Reprinted from *The Remarriage Checkup* by Ron L. Deal and David H. Olson. Used with permission.

5. A. D. Hart, C. H. Weber, and D. Taylor, *Secrets of Eve: Understanding the Mystery of Female Sexuality* (Nashville, TN: Word, 1998).

Chapter 3: Understanding Her Kids (Part 1): Loss

1. Marjorie Smith, "Resident Mothers in Stepfamilies," *The International Handbook of Stepfamilies: Policy and Practice in Legal, Research, and Clinical Environments*, ed. Jan Pryor (Hoboken, NJ: John Wiley & Sons, 2008), 156.

Chapter 4: Understanding Her Kids (Part 2): Loyalty

1. Dave Hahn, "The Everest FAQ Answers," *MountainZone.com*, http://classic.mountainzone.com/everest/99/north/faq6.html.

2. John Bowlby, *A Secure Base: Parent-Child Attachment and Healthy Human Development* (New York: Basic Books, 1988).

3. Bill Doherty, DVD presentation *Working with Remarried Couples in Stepfamilies*, available at *www.drbilldoherty.org*.

4. Ibid.

Chapter 5: Mom Smart (Part 1): He Can't Do It Without You

1. Bill Doherty, DVD presentation *Working with Remarried Couples in Stepfamilies*, available at *www.drbilldoherty.org*.

2. For research references, see "The Elephant in the Bedroom: Cohabi-

tation, Remarriage, and What's Best for Your Relationship," *www .successfulstepfamilies.com/view/376.*

3. Adapted from Susan Gamache, "Parental Status: A new construct describing adolescent perceptions of stepfathers" (PhD diss., University of British Columbia, 2000).

4. For a complete discussion of these factors, see *The Smart Stepfamily* by Ron L. Deal.

5. Lawrence Ganong and Marilyn Coleman, "Adolescent stepchild-stepparent relationships: Changes over time" in Kay Pasley and Marilyn Ihinger-Tallman, eds., *Stepparenting Issues in Theory, Research, and Practice* (Westport, CT: Greenwood Press, 1994), 87–104.

6. Ron L. Deal and David H. Olson, *The Remarriage Checkup: Tools to Help Your Marriage Last a Lifetime,* chapter 7.

Chapter 6: Mom Smart (Part 2): Pitfalls and Good Intentions

1. E. M. Hetherington and W. G. Clingempeel, "Coping with marital transitions: A family systems perspective," *Monographs of the Society for Research in Child Development,* 57, no. 227 (1992).

2. James H. Bray and John Kelly, *Stepfamilies: Love, Marriage, and Parenting in the First Decade* (New York: Broadway, 1998).

3. Lawrence H. Ganong and Marilyn Coleman, *Stepfamily Relationships: Development, Dynamics, and Interventions* (New York: Kluwer Academic/Plenum Publishers, 2004).

4. Marjorie Smith, "Resident Mothers in Stepfamilies," *The International Handbook of Stepfamilies: Policy and Practice in Legal, Research, and Clinical Environments,* ed. Jan Pryor, 162.

5. Gil Stuart, personal communication (January 2010).

Chapter 7: Getting the Socks Picked Up: Parenting 101

1. Marjorie Smith, "Resident Mothers in Stepfamilies," *The International Handbook of Stepfamilies: Policy and Practice in Legal, Research, and Clinical Environments,* ed., Jan Pryor, 159.

2. Jane Nelson, *Positive Discipline* (New York: Ballantine Books, 1996).

3. Gary Chapman, *The Five Love Languages* (Chicago: Northfield Publishing, 1992).

4. Kevin Leman, *Making Children Mind Without Losing Yours* (Grand Rapid, MI: Revell, 2000).

5. Concept from George Doub, Virginia Morgan Scott, and Flo Creighton, *Survival Skills for Healthy Families* and *Survival Skills for Healthy Christian Families* (Salida, CA: Family Wellness Associates, 2008), 59.

Chapter 8: Meet Your Ex-Husband-in-Law: Friend or Foe?

1. L. K. White and J. G. Gilbreth, "When children have two fathers: Effects of relationships with stepfathers and noncustodial fathers on adolescent outcomes," *Journal of Marriage and Family*, 63 (2001): 155–167.

2. Lawrence H. Ganong and Marilyn Coleman, *Stepfamily Relationships: Development, Dynamics, and Interventions* (New York: Kluwer Academic Plenum Publishers, 2004), 49.

3. Ken R. Canfield, PhD, *The 7 Secrets of Effective Fathers* (Carol Stream, IL: Tyndale, 1992).

4. F. F. Furstenberg Jr., and C. W. Nord, "Parenting apart: Patterns of childrearing after marital disruption," *Journal of Marriage and the Family*, 47 (1985): 893–904, as reported in Lawrence H. Ganong and Marilyn Coleman, *Stepfamily Relationships: Development, Dynamics, and Interventions*, 46.

5. James H. Bray and John Kelly, *Stepfamilies: Love, Marriage, and Parenting in the First Decade* (New York: Broadway Books, 1998), 212.

6. Ibid., 236.

7. Ibid., 213, 223–238.

8. Ibid., 214.

9. Ron L. Deal and Laura Petherbridge, *The Smart Stepmom: Practical Steps to Help You Thrive!* (Minneapolis: Bethany House, 2009), 166–167.

10. Adapted from Milton Jones, *How to Love Someone You Can't Stand* (Joplin, MO: College Press, 1997).

Chapter 9: Your Kids: What Do They Need?

1. B. J. Palisi, M. Orleans, D. Caddell, and B. Korn, "Adjustment to stepfatherhood: The effects of marital history and relations with children," *Journal of Divorce & Remarriage* 14 (1991): 89–106.

2. L. K. White and J. G. Gilbreth, "When children have two fathers: Effects of relationships with stepfathers and noncustodial fathers on adolescent outcomes," *Journal of Marriage and Family* 63 (2001): 155–167.

3. E. M. Hetherington and M. M. Stanley-Hagan, "Stepfamilies," *Parenting and Child Development in "Nontraditional" Families*, ed., M. E. Lamb (Mahwah, NJ: Lawrence Erlbaum, 1999), 137–159.

4. James H. Bray and John Kelly, *Stepfamilies: Love, Marriage, and Parenting in the First Decade*, 214.

5. Susan D. Stewart, "Nonresident mothers' and fathers' social contact with children," *Journal of Marriage and the Family*, 61 (1999): 894–907.

6. See Paul Amato and J.G. Gilbreth, "Nonresident fathers and children's wellbeing: A meta-analysis," *Journal of Marriage and the Family* 61 (1999): 557–573, and Susan D. Stewart, "Nonresident parenting and adolescent adjustment: The quality of nonresident father-child interaction," *Journal of Family Issues*, 24 (2003): 217–244.

7. Amato and Gilbreth, 557–573.

Chapter 10: Hugging Your Stepdaughter, Stepsibling Attractions, and the Awkward Issues of Stepfamily Sexuality

1. Marjorie Smith, "Resident Mothers in Stepfamilies," *The International Handbook of Stepfamilies: Policy and Practice in Legal, Research, and Clinical Environments*, ed., Jan Pryor, 159.

2. An excellent resource is Stephen Arterburn and Fred Stoeker with Mike Yorkey, *Every Man's Battle: Winning the War on Sexual Temptation One Victory at a Time* (Colorado Springs, CO: WaterBrook Press, 2009).

3. J. Giles-Sims, "Current Knowledge About Child Abuse in Stepfamilies," *Stepfamilies: History, Research, and Policy*, eds., M. Sussman and I. Levin (New York: The Haworth Press, 1997).

4. I recommend Robert Lewis' resources on Raising a Modern-day Knight. Visit *www.familylife.com*.

Chapter 11: Keeping Special Days Special: Holidays, Vacations, and Your Stepfamily

1. Patricia L. Papernow, "A Clinician's View of 'Stepfamily Architecture': Strategies for Meeting the Challenges," *The International Handbook of Stepfamilies: Policy and Practice in Legal, Research, and Clinical Environments*, ed., Jan Pryor (Hoboken, NJ: John Wiley & Sons, 2008), 443.

Chapter 12: Romancing Your Wife

1. My thanks to author and friend Laura Petherbridge, who contributed to an early version of this chapter.

2. Ron L. Deal and David H. Olson, *The Remarriage Checkup.*

3. See Mike and Harriet McManus, *Living Together: Myths, Risks, and Answers,* (Howard Books, 2008).

4. Adapted from Gary and Barbara Rosberg, *Divorce-Proof Your Marriage* (Wheaton, IL: Tyndale House, 2002), 247–248.

5. Dennis and Barbara Rainey, *Starting Your Marriage Right: What You Need to Know and Do in the Early Years to Make It Last a Lifetime* (Nashville: Thomas Nelson, 2000), 127–129.

6. Ibid., 129.

Chapter 13: Adult Stepchildren

1. For more information about a Shared Covenant, see Greg S. Pettys, "When and How to Use a Shared Covenant Agreement in a Christian Remarriage," *Successful Stepfamilies, www.SuccessfulStepfamilies .com/view/577.*

2. Terri P. Smith with James M. Harper, *When Your Parent Remarries Late in Life: Making Peace With Your Adult Stepfamily* (Avon, MA: Adams Media, 2007).

3. Anne C. Bernstein, *Yours, Mine, and Ours: How Families Change When Remarried Couples Have a Child Together* (New York: Scribner's, 1989).

Chapter 14: Should We Have an "Ours" Baby?

1. L. H. Ganong and M. Coleman, *Remarried Family Relationships* (Thousand Oaks, CA: Sage Publications, 1994).

2. Susan D. Stewart, *Brave New Stepfamilies: Diverse Paths Toward Stepfamily Living* (Thousand Oaks, CA: Sage Publications, 2007), 62–64.

3. A. C. Bernstein, "Stepfamilies from siblings' perspectives," *Marriage & Family Review* 26 (1997): 153–175.

4. A. C. Bernstein, *Yours, Mine, and Ours* (New York: Scribner's, 1989).

5. Susan D. Stewart, *Brave New Stepfamilies: Diverse Paths Toward Stepfamily Living,* 62–64.

6. W. R. Beer, *Strangers in the House: The World of Stepsiblings and Half-siblings* (New Brunswick, NJ: Transaction, 1989).

7. Kay Pasley and Emily Lipe, "How Does Having a Mutual Child Affect Stepfamily Adjustment?" *Stepfamilies* (Summer 1998). View at *www .stepfamilies.info/*.

8. S.D. Stewart, "How the birth of a child affects involvement with stepchildren," *Journal of Marriage and Family*, 67 (2005): 461–473.

9. Anne-Marie Ambert, *Ex-Spouses and New Spouses: A Study of Relationships* (Greenwich, CT: JAI, 1989), chapter 15.

Chapter 15: Heroes by Choice

1. "He Didn't Have to Be" written by Kelley Lovelace and Brad Paisley. © 1999 EMI April Music Inc., Love Ranch Music, and Sea Gayle Music. All Rights Controlled and Administered by EMI April Music Inc. (ASCAP). All Rights Reserved. International Copyright Secured. Quoted from *He Didn't Have to Be*, 2001, Nashville: Rutledge Hill Press, 6.

ABOUT THE AUTHOR

Ron L. Deal is the founder of Successful Stepfamilies, which empowers stepfamilies toward healthy living and equips churches to minister to their unique needs. He is author of *The Smart Stepfamily* and coauthor with Laura Petherbridge of *The Smart Stepmom* and with David H. Olson of *The Remarriage Checkup*. Ron is a licensed marriage and family therapist and licensed professional counselor who frequently appears in the national media, including *Focus on the Family*, *HomeWord*, and *FamilyLife Today*. He is a popular conference speaker and his video series *The Smart Stepfamily DVD* is used in communities, churches, and homes throughout the world. Ron is a member of the Stepfamily Expert Council for the National Stepfamily Resource Center. Ron and his wife, Nan, and their sons live in Amarillo, Texas.

For more about Ron and his ministry, visit *SuccessfulStepfamilies.com*.

More Smart Stepfamily Help from

Expert Ron L. Deal!

A Roadmap for Stepfamilies
Providing practical, realistic solutions to the unique issues that stepfamilies face, Ron Deal helps remarried and soon-to-be married couples solve the everyday puzzles of stepparenting, offering seven steps to raising a healthy family.

The Smart Stepfamily by Ron L. Deal

Just for Stepmoms!
Because the role of stepmom can be confusing and lonely, Ron Deal teams up with experienced stepmom Laura Petherbridge to offer the hope, encouragement, and practical advice women need to survive *and thrive* as a stepmom.

The Smart Stepmom by Ron L. Deal and Laura Petherbridge

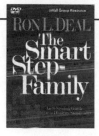

DVD Small-Group Resource
These eight sessions support *The Smart Stepfamily* book and are ideal for small groups or seminars. Deal's personable presentation combines instruction and encouragement, offering useable solutions and tips for everyday living. Also includes a downloadable Participant/Leader Guide.

The Smart Stepfamily Small Group DVD Resource

Vital Remarriage Advice from Stepfamily Experts
Based on research of 50,000+ remarried couples, Ron Deal and marriage expert David H. Olson offer a customizable marriage book specifically for remarried couples. With a free online relationship assessment, this book gives couples customized advice for their relationship and time-tested counsel on issues specific to remarriage.

The Remarriage Checkup by Ron L. Deal and David H. Olson